52 Original Wisdom Stories

Penelope Wilcock is the author of "The Hawk and the Dove" novels and many other books. She has years of experience as a Methodist minister and has worked as a hospice and school chaplain. She has five adult daughters and lives in Hastings, East Sussex. She blogs regularly at *kindredofthequietway.blogspot.com*.

By the same author

Non-fiction

100 Stand-Alone Bible Studies
In Celebration of Simplicity
The Road of Blessing
The Wilderness Within You
Learning to Let Go
Spiritual Care of Dying and Bereaved People

Fiction

The Hawk and the Dove
The Wounds of God
The Long Fall
The Hardest Thing to Do
The Hour Before Dawn
Remember Me
The Breath of Peace
Thereby Hangs a Tale
The Clear Light of Day
Urban Angel (with Stewart Henderson)

52

Original Wisdom Stories

Short lively pieces for the Christian year

Penelope Wilcock

MONARCH
BOOKS

Oxford, UK & Grand Rapids, Michigan, USA

Published by Monarch Books
an imprint of
Lion Hudson plc
Wilkinson House, Jordan Hill Road,
Oxford OX2 8DR, England
Email: monarch@lionhudson.com
www.lionhudson.com/monarch

ISBN 978 0 85721 602 1
e-ISBN 978 0 85721 603 8

First edition 2015

Acknowledgments
Unless otherwise noted, Scripture quotations are taken from The Authorized (King James) Version. Rights in the Authorized Version are vested in the Crown. Reproduced by permission of the Crown's patentee, Cambridge University Press.

Scripture quotations marked NKJV are taken from the New King James Version. Copyright © 1982 by Thomas Nelson, Inc. Used by permission. All right reserved.

Scripture quotations marked ESV are from The Holy Bible, English Standard Version® (ESV®) copyright © 2001 by Crossway, a publishing ministry of Good News Publishers. All rights reserved.

Scripture quotations marked NIV are taken from the *Holy Bible, New International Version*, copyright © 1973, 1978, 1984 International Bible Society. Used by permission of Hodder & Stoughton, a member of the Hodder Headline Group. All rights reserved. "NIV" is a trademark of International Bible Society. UK trademark number 1448790.

Scripture quotations marked NLT are taken from the *Holy Bible, New Living Translation*, copyright © 1996, 2004, 2007 by Tyndale House Foundation. Used by permission of Tyndale House Publishers, Inc., Carol Stream, Illinois 60188. All rights reserved.

Scripture quotations marked NRSV are from The New Revised Standard Version of the Bible copyright © 1989 by the Division of Christian Education of the National Council of Churches in the USA. Used by permission. All Rights Reserved.

A catalogue record for this book is available from the British Library

Printed and bound in the UK, June 2015, LH36

For Pearl Thornton, with my love

Contents

Foreword

I was for some years a tutor for trainee local preachers in the Methodist Church. When it came to writing a sermon, there were questions to be borne in mind:

- How will this build the faith of the hearers?
- Where is the Good News in what I have said?

And, crucially:

- How does it help make a bridge linking contemporary living and the eternal gospel?

In writing this book I have asked the same questions.

I have particularly tried to address three issues I believe urgently require attention from the church of today.

Firstly, I wanted to look at the phenomenon of what I have come across described as "the Dones". That is, Christian people – committed, faithful, believing, many of whom have held responsible leadership positions – who, for one reason or another, are absolutely done with church. They don't go any more. They have not left the church, they are still part of it, but they are no longer church*goers*. This group of people is increasing, and it should cause us to look long and hard at what we now mean by membership of the church. What does it mean to belong to the household of faith but not attend public worship? The format of this book is a series of conversations between a fictional husband and wife couple, Sid and Rosie. Both of them have stopped attending the mainstream church. One has become a Quaker, the other attends here and there, now and then. But both of them are serious believers. They offer us an opportunity to ask ourselves some questions about the growing segment of the church they represent. Another thing about Sid and Rosie is that both of them take marriage seriously but both are divorced and remarried. They offer us the opportunity to consider the situation now facing us – almost every family we know includes members who have been through divorce; yet we know Christian marriage is a blessing of God and a good foundation for sane and healthy family life. What ethical Christian framework can we work out that honestly recognizes our situation, and shapes a compassionate, realistic discipline of life that does not rely on putting its head in the sand?

Secondly, the church must get to grips with the immense spiritual implications of climate change. Serious scientists are talking about the year 2030 as a tipping point, and are saying we have now passed the point of no return: the human race can expect perhaps 100 years of life left, in conditions of increasing scarcity and environmental degradation. Crafting a theology of hope and compassion for the years ahead is perhaps the most vital task of today's church. This book offers a number of opportunities to engage with the issues raised.

Thirdly, the church is changing. Cathedral worship attendance is increasing, informal home-based church is increasing (in Iran, for example), and community churches (like NewFrontiers and Kings Church) are increasing, even as church as we once knew it is still dwindling in numbers (though often vital and satisfying in any particular individual congregation). The changes in form have many implications, one being that those attending worship in the newer manifestations of church may have no experience or understanding of the old liturgical structures – their meaning, purpose and origin. Why does this matter? Because the traditional structure of the ecclesiastical year gave a rounded education in the life of Christ and the themes of the gospel, whereas an unstructured year brings a strong risk of the importation of a "personal canon" – emphasis on the pet preoccupations of the pastor. This book works through the main fasts and feasts of the traditional ecclesiastical year, including some of the feasts of our most beloved and significant saints (not all). It also identifies the ecclesiastical feasts of the ancient Celtic church (pre-Council of Whitby) and explains how they were built upon the rhythms of the pre-Christian agricultural year. This in turn offers us a fascinating glimpse into a non-confrontational method of evangelism – one that takes no adversarial stance towards the receiving culture, but that works with it to gently illuminate what is already there with the light and hope of the gospel.

The book can be used for personal devotion or public reading in small groups and church services. My prayer is that it may achieve its objectives of building your faith; revealing the Good News and the vital, essential importance it must play in the context of increasing fragmentation in the modern world; building a bridge between contemporary living and the eternal truth of the gospel; and deepening understanding concerning the nature and purpose of the structure of the ecclesiastical year.

Pen Wilcock
November 2014

1

Advent 1 – The Beginning

"An oak tree," said Sid, "grows for 300 years, rests for 300 years, and takes 300 years to die."

Comfortable in his battered easy chair, his gaze rests peacefully on the glowing embers and falling ash of the fire at the end of this long, dark November evening. The wind blusters and gusts round the roof and walls of this old house.

Rosie – Sid's wife – hunts in the pile of wools beside her for her scissors. She wants to change colour. She can bite through the yarn she's on at the moment, but is familiar with the feeling of small wool fibres impossible to get out of her mouth afterwards, and doesn't like it. "That's a long time," she says, absently. She feels behind her – ah! There they are. "300 years. It sounds kind of… sad."

"The dying part?"

"Yes."

"Well, I know what you mean," says Sid, "but in reality it's full of surprising hope and regeneration. In its dying, an oak tree not only feeds on itself – consumes its own nutrients – it sustains a whole fantastic range of other living beings as well: beetles and all manner of wriggly things and little creeps. That's how it is with a tree. A wise man said, although in a forest you can see fallen trees, decaying stumps and leaf mould, it's more truly metamorphosis than death. He[1] said, 'Death is not the opposite of life. Life has no opposite. The

1   Eckhart Tolle, *A New Earth*, Penguin, 2005.

opposite of death is birth. Life is eternal.' It's an ouroboros."

Rosie looks up from her crochet. "Come again?"

Sid chuckles. "Don't you know that word? The snake that swallows its own tail. It's a really ancient symbol. Big. Big in meaning, that is. It can represent primordial unity. Or it can be like the phoenix rising from the ashes – 'In my end is my beginning.' It represents something – life, prāṇa, ch'i, the Tao, the Holy Spirit; whatever you call it – that exists with no identifiable beginning, and persists with such intrinsic power that it cannot be destroyed. Like the light that shines in the darkness, and the darkness can neither comprehend nor extinguish it.[2] It just goes on."

Rosie frowns at her pile of yarns, trying to decide between two greens. It goes well with purple, but if you don't get the shade right it looks garish.

"Right... " She hopes she sounds encouraging. "And the oak tree... er..."

Sid smiles. He knows she is indulging him, but without someone to at least pretend to listen to his thoughts, he would be lonely.

"It's not the oak tree, it's the life in the oak tree. Life persists like an ouroboros – it cannot be lost. It has no end and no beginning. It is eternal. The old Celts knew about it. The quarter days and cross-quarter days of the Celtic agricultural year track it. Before the church went over to the Roman way of doing things after the Council of Whitby, the ecclesiastical year, modelled an ouroboros, told the story of eternal life."

The sage green is best, the quiet grey-green with its pure, silvery tone. It lets the purple sing. That brighter hue makes it shout. She joins the new yarn to the old end.

"Oh, right? And we're just coming to the end of the cycle, then."

"No. Yes. No."

She glances up at him over the rim of her glasses, amused. "Make up your mind!"

---

2   John 1:5 (my paraphrase of all translations).

"Well – " Sid is hesitant, not because he is unsure but because he cares about this. Eagerness steals into his voice. If he starts to tell her about this, he wants to be heard, to really be able to say it. He looks at her. Rosie is listening.

"The thing about the Celtic day," he explains, "is that it doesn't begin in the morning. It starts at sundown – like the Jewish sabbath, I guess. So the old Celts, who rated dreams highly – also like the ancient Jews – believed our dreams were not us processing the day gone but preparing for the day coming. And as with the day, so with the year. The Celtic year starts as the sun goes down, not as it rises. Yul, 'the turn' (it's an old Viking word), marks the moment when the infant light is born, and the year turns towards the light. So, that's like the year's dawn. And the year ends with Samhain, the day of the dead. When the Irish missionaries brought the gospel, they didn't try to overthrow the old ways, they worked with them, saw wisdom in them. So they settled the feast of All Saints on the day of the dead. It was a special time, what the Celts called a thin time, when the veil between the everyday world and the realm of weird became diaphanous. On that day, the people remembered their ancestors, those they had loved and who had taught them wisdom and truth. The people they belonged to who had passed into the unseen world. So it made sense to set All Saints on that day of observance. And of course, they made Yul – the turn, the birth of the infant light – into the feast of the Incarnation; the baby Jesus, light of the world.

"But then, what about the space between the end of the year at Samhain and the dawn of the new year at Yul? Oh, Rosie, this is where it gets exciting! It's so *interesting*!"

She smiles at his enthusiasm – this is one of the things she loves about Sid. "Go on," she says. "I'm crocheting, but I'm listening too."

"Well, after Samhain comes No-Time. You know I said about the oak tree growing, then resting, then dying? You know how there are different stages of labour when a baby is born – the first stage opens up the womb, the second stage is the power rush of pushing energy, but between them comes a nameless hiatus of deep rest?[3] Well, No-Time is like that hiatus, the nameless space in the giving of life; and, in the turning year, the space between death and life. It's not clear how long exactly No-Time lasted, but remember the Celtic day starts with evening. No-Time is the evening that begins the coming year. The Irish missionaries settled Advent on it. Advent is the evening with which the new year begins."

"So… the new year isn't January the first?"

"No. Yul is the turn, and we celebrate the Incarnation then; but the beginning is this bit, the evening of the year's day. And the church made Advent a time to look forward to the coming of Christ the King. In Advent they focused on both the coming of the baby at Bethlehem – the infant Light born in deepest darkness – and the coming of Christ in glory, as judge. Do you see, by doing this they crowned Christ King of the all-important circle of the Celtic agricultural year. They were farmers, it meant everything to them. The missionaries built it right into their pattern of life, the implication: 'Jesus is Lord'.

"No-Time, where we are now, the year holds its breath, looks forward to the new. The old is gone and the new has not yet begun. The Celtic day starts with evening, and that's why Advent, at the end of the old year, is the beginning of the church's year. This is where we enter the ouroboros, because this is the end, the year is dying, going down into its deepest darkness, its oblivion. But in its end is its beginning. So because this is the end, and life is eternal, forever renewing itself – this is the beginning."

For sharing and wondering

- Describe your favourite trees.
- What have been the really big beginnings and endings in your life?
- When you think about dying – your own death, or the death of people close to you –what sort of feelings are stirred up?

3   Sheila Kitzinger described this hiatus as "rest and be thankful".

Into the Mystery

Eternal God, source of all that is, your being is the only power, your grace runs through the cosmos, the life-giving blood, the rising sap. So steep us in the quietness of your presence that our little lives may attain the stability and peace of your wisdom, your love, your truth.

2

Advent 2 – Harrowing Hell

Sid gets up early. Some mornings, like today, he tiptoes downstairs quietly to avoid waking Rosie. He sleeps on the floor, a lifelong habit, so he doesn't disturb her as he steals silently out of their bedroom – because Rosie has no intention of giving up her comfy bed for anyone.

This morning he is headed for the bathroom. Sid knows he should take showers: they use much less water, it's more ecologically responsible. He feels guilty about it, but he just can't make himself give up his long soak in a deep, hot bath. He doesn't take one every day; he rations himself. Every other day, and just a sponge-bath on the days in between.

It's dark, but Sid doesn't switch on the overhead light in the bathroom. He brings his camping lantern with him – it's what he has for a bedside lamp. The light it sheds is adequate but not bright, just enough to be able to see what he's doing. He puts it right down in the corner there, on the floor alongside the toilet.

The reason Sid prefers the bathroom not too bright is that he loves to watch the dawn light come. He opens the window even though it's chilly, so he can hear the first of the day's birdsong – a seagull's cry, the thread of song from a robin, the chirping of a sparrow.

He runs the bath right up to the overflow as hot as he can stand, and luxuriates in the relaxing warmth and the spicy, herbal, aromatic scent of the bubbles. He lies back, resting his head on the edge of the tub, and he watches the rising day gradually displacing the shadows. The bathroom windows are fitted with obscured glass – otherwise he and his next-door neighbour would be greeted by an eyeful of greater intimacy than either would prefer – but the opacity doesn't diminish the beauty of the sunrise, the pink and golden light gradually filling the room with glory. Sid loves this. It never loses its magic, however often he comes creeping stealthily down the stairs for his date with the beauty and wonder of the dawning day.

At this time of year, still dark when he gets in the bath, his camping lantern is a necessary light. By the time he gets out and reaches for his towel the lamp is redundant; day has come.

This morning as he drifts and dreams in the comforting, soapy warmth, Sid thinks about a tenet of the church's creeds that has always seemed opaque to him: "He descended into hell." What does that mean? Sid wonders. What is its implication?

Does it mean that Jesus in focused manner parried his adversary – plundered the HQ of the opposing forces? Does it just mean Jesus fell… and fell… and fell… out of consciousness, out of vitality, out of anything we could think of as being, into the deepest, darkest cold imaginable – into the icy fastness of spiritual winter? What did it mean, for Jesus? And equally, what did it mean for hell?

Sid imagines Jesus taken down by the courage of his love, his self-sacrifice, into the power of death. He thinks of Jesus carried by God into the darkness – the bowels of the Earth, the lostness of death, beyond all hope or feeling, beyond pulse or breath… gone. Sid thinks of God carrying Jesus down into the dark; "the true Light, which lighteth every man that cometh into the world…"[4]

"In him was life; and the life was the light of men. And the light shineth in darkness; and the darkness comprehended it not…"[5] And Sid wonders what happened next. Light, he thinks, cannot die. The light of Jesus was never lost because its nature was love. It lived

4   John 1:9.
5   John 1:4–5.

on in the sorrow of loss, in lives healed and transformed, in people who would never be the same again because they had known Jesus. Prostitutes given back their dignity. Lepers given back their place in the community. Demoniacs given back sanity and peace. Inherent in the love of Jesus was new beginning. And it was loose in the world, intrinsically and unstoppably alive.

So when he died, descended into hell – what then? Only the body dies, and that lay mute and silent in the grave. Like a seed in winter, Sid thinks, lying silent in the harrowed ground. But the soul of Jesus – his living spirit – where did that go? If he went down to hell, then he went as a light into darkness.

Sid imagines the wise and royal soul of Jesus – noble, gentle, bent on compassion – finding the way down the twisty, broken gap-tooth stair to the lonely pit of hell. The black place where joy shrivels like a fallen winter leaf, where all laughter is finished and songs die on the lips and are heard no more.

"He was in the world, and the world was made by him, and the world knew him not…"[6] He pitched his tent among us. He bivouacked among us. He brought his light here, where it was so dark without him. He lent his light to us who needed it so much.

Sid can almost see it. The quiet, purposeful descent into the final darkness. Everything else done but this one last task – searching out the souls who were lost and forgotten. The light himself climbing down into nether darkness. The Word of God climbing down into the dumb place of the silenced and outcast. He brought them light.

He stayed there, like Sid's camping lantern in its dusty corner down beside the toilet, being the light in this night of abandonment. But this was *Jesus* – not an LED bulb running on three AA batteries. This was living light. The light seed. The original whisper of the Logos – "Let there be light". The light in Jesus was the light of the making, that begot the world's morning, that sang into being the principle of dawn.

6   John 1:10.

Thus was hell harrowed, by the light seed falling down, down into the icy winter earth, consenting to stay there until light shone all around – until not the light, but hell itself, became redundant.

Sid has no idea if this bears any resemblance to what really happened to Jesus. But he thinks it actually must do, because something of this nature happened within his own hell, within his own hopeless heart, when the light seed of the presence of Jesus by God's grace took root within him, and brought to life again so much that had been trashed and trampled. Brought him hope again. And, eventually, his Rosie.

Day has come and the bath is no more than lukewarm. Sid hooks out the plug with his toe, and feels over the edge of the bath for his big fluffy towel.

For sharing and wondering

- What's your morning routine?
- How do your mind and body fare in the months of winter darkness?
- Can you think of an incident from your own life that was an experience of redemption?

Into the Mystery

In you, O God, we find the treasures of darkness and the light of life. In those times and seasons when our lives descend into the darkness of sorrow or struggle, please come down and find us, stay with us. Then, when the time is right, lead us up into the hope of new possibilities.

3

Advent 3 – The Missing Jesus

This kind of shop does Sid's head in. The only possibility of movement is cautiously edging past other customers along the narrow walkway left between the display shelves lining the walls and the massive, cluttered edifice of wares towering the length of the centre space. Porcelain, fluffy toys, Turkish lanterns, handbags, high-end toiletries, greetings cards, ornaments, make-up, special occasion gift trinkets, silk scarves, vases, party games, stationery, candlesticks, gloves, artificial flowers and jewellery all compete dangerously for the limited space. Nothing gives an inch. Everything clamours for attention. Sid can see absolutely nothing useful here. No mole wrenches. No screen wash. Not even socks.

At this season of the year, a series of fake Christmas trees of varying size have been shoe-horned into the centre display. You can tell they are Christmas trees by the shape, but the branches can only just be glimpsed through the jostle of baubles, rinky-dinky reindeer in a multitude of cutesy representations, and Perspex icicles. He cannot fathom how Rosie can browse here with such nonchalance, pausing to stroke the ears of a creamy-white, ultra-fluffy toy bunny, peering intently into the cabinet of earrings – turquoise, garnet, peridot, abalone, amethyst, coral, labradorite; she loves them. What to him blurs into a suffocating Mammon-fest of get-me-out-of-here, delights and fascinates Rosie.

She pauses, bending over a group of rustic ceramic Nativity

figures grouped at the foot of a small Christmas tree bristling with ornaments and heavily encrusted with spray-on snow. She looks… looks again… straightens up and asks no one in particular, "Where's Jesus?"

Where indeed, thinks Sid, but evidently that's not what she means. The chic, slender, vivacious sales assistant sashays out from behind the counter with its gift wrap and tumble of sticky tape, last-minute tempters, pens and order lists. Her wide smile crosses the tiny space to join Rosie beside the crib scene.

"He was stolen," she explains in her delightful Italian accent that seems not just foreign but exotic in this cornucopia of a bazaar. "Somebody took him, last year."

Rosie is staring at the woman, her expression unreadable. The saleslady feels it incumbent upon her to explain further.

"We thought – you know – it would be easy to just make something, get something else from somewhere, to put in instead," she says, with an engaging little shrug, tipping her head to one side. Moving the conversation on from lingering on anything that could be construed as a possible deficiency in her shop, she begins to make conversation. "They have lots of these in Italy," she offers. "They are a really big thing there – in some places they are more important than the actual tree!"

Rosie is boggling now, gazing at the salesclerk in fascinated astonishment. "The Nativity? It has become more important than the tree?" she echoes, hardly able to believe what she has just heard.

Though they are standing in such intimate proximity in the miniscule patch of well-trodden ground just within the doorway of this gift shop, there arises the odd sense that somehow they have managed to import two entirely different worlds. Rosie pulls herself together and looks round for Sid. "Shall we go upstairs for a cup of coffee?" she asks him. Not a square inch of space is wasted in this emporium. Upstairs they sell coffee and a selection of delectable cakes. Sid readily falls in with this proposal, and the sales assistant is satisfied with their polite withdrawal from her attention. They are, after all, going to buy something, even if it's only a cappuccino.

"I can't believe I just heard what that woman said." Rosie takes off her gloves and sinks into a chair at the table they bagged by the window. Sid hangs his jacket on the back of another chair, and goes across to the counter to place their order. Jasmine tea for Rosie, an Americano and a hunk of that rich fruit cake for him.

"About someone stealing Jesus?" he picks up again, returning to sit with her and wait for the barista to bring their order. "I believe it does happen. A sweet little baby. Catches someone's fancy. Easy to slip into a purse."

"Oh, I know," says Rosie, "but that's not what I meant. In the first place, how could anyone even countenance the notion for five minutes that it might be OK to go ahead with a crib scene *that has no Jesus*? What does she think? Jesus is just *incidental* – might as well have been the ox or the little lamb? Everything else is in place, what does it matter if Jesus is there or not? Jeepers! Is that a parable for our day or is the Pope not a Catholic?

"And then that weird business about some places in Italy the nativities have more prominence than the tree. Dash it all, Sid, the woman's Italian – she must know Italy is a Catholic country… or was… or… It's where the Vatican is… More important than *the tree*? Er, *yes*, I should think so!"

"Well, it's theological." Sid smiles up at the cheery waitress who brings their drinks and his mouth-watering (and colossal) wedge of cake, all moist with glistening fruit. "Thank you!" He waits until she has arranged their bits and pieces and flicked away to her next task.

"It's a question that has been hotly contended over millennia," he says. "Which was more important, the crib or the tree – Christmas or Easter? Some people say Easter is the clear winner, death defeated and the power of sin broken for good and all. Christ triumphant, victor over the grave. How could that not be the pinnacle of the Christian year? A new creation. But for all that, it's Christmas not Easter that has caught the imagination and won the hearts of ordinary people. Christ not in his strength and power but in all his vulnerability and frailty, the homeless baby in the manger, the animals and the ordinary people the only ones who witnessed it. Emmanuel, God with us. People in the ordinary struggle of daily life find it easier to relate to, than either the flayed and tortured man with his death that cost everything, or the incomprehensible miracle of Easter morning. The crib or the tree? Which matters the most?"

Rosie sniffs the fragrance of her jasmine tea with appreciation as she raises the cup to drink.

"I think they've solved the problem for all eternity downstairs in that shop," she says. "Somebody's stolen Jesus, and they don't think it really matters. All there is left is a fake tree encrusted with fake icicles and fake snow, and a fake Mary with her hands crossed on her fake chest, on her stoneware knees gazing in adoration and devotion at a very small empty space. The tree or the crib scene – what does it matter? He isn't there. All that's left is a pile of tat and a season meaning enough sales to keep the enterprise back from the edge of bankruptcy one more year. If Jesus hadn't been stolen from here, he would have been sold. '*More than the actual tree!*' What have we come to, Sid?"

He smiles at her. "I don't think he minds," he says. "At least she thought to include a Nativity scene in her stock. And even if people have lost touch with what it was originally all about, there is generosity at this time of year, and parties, and treats for the children. There are shoeboxes of gifts packed and sent to Romania, lunches put on for homeless and lonely people, night shelters open and a few extras put into the food bank collection box at the back of the grocery store. I think Jesus can work with that. And I wonder who it was stole the little baby from the crib scene? They'd displayed it at just about the height for a small child. Maybe there's a little kiddie somewhere with a guilty secret – concealing their stolen Jesus, getting him out to gaze and adore when no one is looking.

24

Somebody must have him, even if he isn't here. *There's* a game for the new year, Rosie! Let's search for the secret Jesus! Let's see if we can discern him, in the lives where he's hidden right away, completely concealed. The unexpected innocence or kindness, the unlooked-for generosity. I wonder where he is, the baby Jesus? It's easy enough to see where he's missing, but where's he hiding? Let's look for him, Rosie. I think that would be really fun. In every person we meet, let's see if we can spot the hidden Jesus!"

For sharing and wondering

- What do you enjoy most about Christmas?
- Which feast best speaks to your own heart – Christmas or Easter – and why?
- Think of some relationships or situations in your own life where you'd like to search for the hidden Jesus.

Into the Mystery

Emmanuel, you are always with us. In every human life, your presence is discernible, if only we have the eyes to see. Give us the grace to find you and love you, even in your most unpromising disguise.

4

Advent 4 – The Judge

"What's on your mind, Sid my love?"

Rosie eyes his pensive face as she opens the new bag of filter coffee. Sid is usually a picture of contentment at breakfast time. He never gets tired of oatmeal with brown sugar and a little cream. He loves the early light and the birdsong of daybreak. Mornings are good. But he is deep in thought today.

"I was thinking," he tells her, "about criminals in court. Or not even just criminals – divorce cases too. I can imagine how your heart must sink if, say, you discover that the judge hearing your case is notoriously racist, or has very traditional views about women's place in society or is very pro fox-hunting or some such thing; and those views will have a bearing on your case. Maybe you have the wrong skin colour or the woman raped was out at 2 a.m. in fishnet stockings and a miniskirt, or you are known to have life membership of the Hunt Saboteurs. It would make a difference, wouldn't it?"

"Yes," Rosie agrees: "I should think it most certainly would."

"And there again," he says, "I've heard mutterings about Freemasons in the dock. Whether this is true or just prejudice against them I cannot say; but I've heard of judicial outcomes supposedly affected by a criminal and a judge being members of the same Lodge. Who knows? It's possible, human nature being what it is."

He eats his last spoonful of porridge, and looks down with vague regret at the empty bowl. But the kitchen is full of the aroma of fresh coffee brewing. Life is full of hope.

"I had a friend," he says, 'who was put through the wringer in a seriously spiteful divorce case. I can't think what got into his wife. I always liked her, and I've no doubt that he's a good man, but somehow she really had it in for him. She absolutely went to town. And his lawyers were a ragtag and bobtail set of ill-prepared mealy-mouthed defeatists. Her people wiped the floor with him. Took him for all he had, plus the change. One hearing especially stuck in my mind, where his obligations of regular financial payments were assessed on the basis of his income – obviously – but they had the gross figure where they should have had the net. The judge was made aware of this – and *he didn't care*! Shrugged it off. Too bad. Tough. It was unjust, and the judge knew it was unjust, but he wasn't interested. I guess judges do get impatient at finding themselves inadvertently roped in to mediation, but... when a judge doesn't care about justice, the system's sunk, isn't it?"

"The system?" says Rosie. "Ha! Tell me about it! Systems snack on the ruined lives of individuals all day long."

Sid looks at her thoughtfully. She has a line of cynicism running through the centre of her soul, not exactly of her own making. It is the accretion of too many experiences of grief and struggle, of being left to get on with situations in which she felt overwhelmed. It has left this dark seam of bitterness running right through the middle of her. Rosie believes in God, but not so much in the goodness of human nature.

"Then I was thinking," he goes on, " how it might be if you were a habitual criminal. If you had been in the clink on and off the whole of your adult life. If magistrates thought you were scum and the police knew all too well where you lived and every detail of your life. If no sooner were you back in circulation than you would have your shoulder to some basement door on a dark night, up to your old tricks again. A thoroughly bad lot. And suppose you were eventually and inevitably arraigned before a judge, and your comeuppance seemed likely to be serious with a capital S this time. No matter how well you knew the form, how often you'd gone through this mill, how many times you'd listen to them tell you what a bit of poison you were and how long you'd be going down for this time – you'd still be dreading it, wouldn't you?

"And then, imagine if the way things turned out, you were allocated a judge who knew you and loved you. Someone who knew all too well about your miserable childhood, the grinding poverty that had shaped and moulded you, the disadvantages in education. Someone who understood how you'd tried as well as how you'd failed. Someone who knew about your kindness to little kiddies and your loyalty to your old mum, your generosity to your friends and your gentleness with your dogs – as well as the petty crime that kept getting you into trouble.

"That would be a turn-up for the books, wouldn't it? To know that the person judging your case that day would be straight with you, would be fair – but also loved you and was 100 per cent on your side."

Rosie considers this. "That seems to me tremendously unlikely," she pronounces.

Sid grins. "All right, then. Suppose it was a divorce case. Suppose it was all in a traditional, rural community where everybody knew everybody else, so you could trust that when your case came up before the judge there'd be none of this irritable dismissal of the facts – because the judge really knew you both as people, and cared properly about what happened to your kids. That would be good, don't you think?"

"What are you doing, Sid?" enquires his wife. "Planning Utopia?"

"Not that," says Sid. "I was just thinking about the Last Judgment. I was thinking that in the course of my life I have made some serious mistakes. I've done some things I have been very, very ashamed of. I've been stupid. I've been mean at times. Sometimes I've meant well but things have come out badly, horribly wrong. And I've also just given up. Thrown in the towel, Stopped trying. Just let everything slide because I ran out of ways to make my life work.

"I was imagining what it would be like, to come before God at the Last Judgment with all that... mess... to answer for. I was picturing it like being a criminal brought handcuffed into the dock, or like a man in the divorce courts waiting to see if he'll actually have enough of his income left to live on, let alone start again, come the end of the afternoon. And then it occurred to me: the judgment of my life will not be handed down from some remote, impervious, indifferent, prejudiced toff. My life will be judged by the one who loves me best in all the world. And, Rosie – I think that must surely make a difference."

For sharing and wondering

- Can you think of a time in your life when you were especially grateful for an unexpected kindness?
- What are your own feelings about the current state of social justice in your country?
- How do you imagine the judgment of God in relation to your own life?

Into the Mystery

Our King and our Judge, you are also our Creator and our Friend. There is no one who understands us better than you, and nobody who loves us more. May the everyday decisions of our lives, and the principles on which we build, be determined by the kindness and unmerited grace of your judgment.

5

Christmas/Yul

"So here were are," says Sid, on this magical night. They are walking through the chill dark, their evening constitutional: twenty minutes round the block of tatty houses in this rundown old town where they live. It's a delight, this night walk. Every few paces a cat slinks quietly out of their path into hidden shelter under a parked car, or watches them gravely, a mound of fur with two pointy ears, on a wall, a windowsill, the tarpaulin covering a car trailer. They are alert for black cats, in the deep shadows where shrubs and tottering garden walls block the shine of the streetlamps and the multi-coloured glow of Christmas lights from the row of houses lining the street. Sometimes the only sign of a black cat is a momentary twin gleam of eyes, and an indefinable movement of dark within dark.

Rosie loves Christmas. She has no time for complex social encounters or gluts of gifts – she stopped buying presents years ago, even for her children, determined to reclaim the peace and wonder of this holy season. As a concession to kindness and understanding, she has purchased one small dinosaur for each of her grandchildren. A Therizinosaurus with spine-chilling claws, and a Postosuchus.

But she wants to focus, really concentrate, on the sense of the year going deeper, deeper, climbing down the stairway into the Earth's night, depths of mystery, when all of creation looks dormant, not because it is asleep but because it is waiting. The season of the watchman.

"I love it," she says, as they stroll along beside the hedges and small gardens of the quiet town empty of people, everyone inside behind the curtained windows of their lamp-lit homes. "I love the terrific sense of anticipation. Everything is so still, all the Earth silent, but it's not the silence of death. It's like the whole earth is watching, holding its breath, because something tremendous is about to happen. The stars are looking down. There's something going on. And tonight – it's the twenty-first, Sid – isn't this the winter solstice?"

"It is indeed," he says. "It always comes between the twentieth and the twenty-third. Tonight is Yul."

"Did you see the card we had from Bente and Aleks? That says *God Jul* on the front. It must be a Scandinavian word."

"Yes, spot on. The Vikings brought it. *Yul* – 'the turn'. In the ancient Celtic agricultural year, it was the turning point; the longest, darkest night, the place where the light-seed appeared – the birth of the infant light that allowed all growth to start again. The cradle of hope and life."

"Oh – and the birthday of Jesus! How wonderful."

But, "No," says Sid. "It's not Jesus' birthday. In Islam they celebrate the birthday of the Prophet and in Buddhism they have Wesak, the birthday of the Buddha, but Christianity doesn't celebrate the birthday of Jesus, because they are looking beyond the man to the meaning. I don't think anyone knows – or really cares – exactly when Jesus was born. It's supposed to be sometime around September. But that's not what Christmas is."

"Oh. What is it then?"

"The feast of the Incarnation. It's those wise and respectful first missionaries of Christianity, harmonizing the light of the gospel with the old pagan religion that followed the Earth's heartbeat, the rhythm of the seasons. They didn't push the old feasts out of the way. They let Yul have its day. But they set Christmas just adjacent to it – a system that says, 'Look; these are the same'."

"It's the celebration of the coming of the Christlight into a world lost in darkness – 'In him was life; and the life was the light of men. And the light shineth in darkness…'[7]

"Jesus, he is the light-seed. In the old pagan understanding, that makes him the king of the farming year, because the Earth is the goddess – the lady – and the sun is the lord, the god. The old pagan religion scries into the wonder and meaning and holy power underlying the turning of the world, seeing it as a connection to what they called the realm of weird – the huge and hidden dimension. So, placing the feast of the Incarnation at Yul is a kind of pictogram of Jesus the Light of the World. It's a credal statement, if you like. It's a way of saying 'Jesus is Lord'. The sun-king, the light-seed, the hope of the Earth."

Rosie looks at the Christmas lights, red, yellow, green, framing the bay windows of the house they are passing.

"That's why we have Christmas lights, then?"

"Well… I guess maybe also because they're effective and look pretty, seeing as it's a dark time of year. But, when I was sitting in Meeting last Sunday, it occurred to me that pure light is white because it contains all the colours. You have to split the light with a prism to see its rainbow, the spectrum. And Quakers speak of God as the Light, saying there is 'that of God in every man' and looking beyond a person's faults and frailties for the light-seed."

"In every man?" Rosie interrupts him. "Not women?"

"I don't think George Fox had got as far as inclusive language. Besides which, in the eighteenth century they were nearer than we are to Middle English and Old English. The word for a person in Old English is 'manne'. The word for a male human is 'were'."

"Ooh! Like a were-wolf!"

"Exactly so. 'Man' wasn't always exclusive. 'Were' and 'wife' was man and woman. 'Manne' was any human being. Anyway, what I was saying about the light of God in every man – it came to me that in

---

7   John 1:4–5.

humanity the pure Light of God splits into its spectrum. Like, some people are gentle and hospitable, some are wise and insightful, some are cunning and quick, some are nurturing, some are contemplative. All different. Aspects of the one Light. And it made me think of a string of Christmas lights, all shining different colours."

"'Cunning' doesn't sound very nice," Rosie comments. "Is God cunning?"

"I meant it in the Old English sense of practical knowledge. Wily, crafty, a pragmatic kind of knowing that's for the everyday; different from the Weird knowledge of the Wise Ones. For the hands-on more than for the prophetic, if you see what I mean."

They turn the corner into their own street, and Rosie pulls her thick woolly cardigan closer around her. "Brrr. It's certainly chilly. There'll be a frost tonight."

As they pass the vets and the bus station, she suddenly laughs.

"You love the history

"And I love the mystery."

"Ha! We are a couplet! We belong together. We were made for each other. We are a rhyming pair."

In the darkness Sid smiles. "Yes," he says, "we surely do belong together. But – I love the mystery too."

"Ah, then," she says, "you must definitely love me. Because I am *extremely* mysterious."

"You can say that again," says Sid.

"I am extremely mysterious," says Rosie, in a tiny, husky little whisper of a voice.

In the shadows between two street lamps, Sid takes her in his arms and kisses her.

For sharing and wondering

- Can you describe your favourite time, place and companion for a walk?

- If we no longer used "darkness" as a metaphor for evil, what other metaphors could we think of?

- If you were asked to make a simple all-age church service to celebrate Christmas, what essential and optional elements might you include?

Into the Mystery

Loving Lord Jesus, our Friend and Brother, our Redemption and our Hope, we thank you so much for coming to do this journey with us, for walking alongside us every day as our companion and wise guide.

6

Feast of the Holy Family – Love Wins

"Love wins." It's what Sid always says, and Rosie tries hard to remember it right now, as she and her defiant grandson glare at each other over the flung-about toys.

Love wins.

"Pick them up," she says. "Please."

"No!" He glares at her. "*You* pick them up!"

"Right now," she says, keeping her voice steady and calm with a certain amount of effort and wondering why this child is always like this, "or they go in the bin."

"No! No! No!"

Yes, she thinks; that seems to be the general gist of his approach to human relationships. She will not give way. The confrontation goes on a few minutes more, then she sweeps up the scattered toys into a rubbish bag while he roars with fury and distress.

Love wins. Does it? Always?

She and Sid have both been married before. They have both brought up children, but not together. Both of them prized domestic peace and defended it, but they did it in different ways. Sid is a diplomat and Rosie a warrior. Rosie kept the peace by setting – and maintaining – clear, firm boundaries and expectations, Sid by going the second mile. Rosie is candid. Sid is kind. "What's he like?" Rosie will ask Sid, about a new acquaintance. "Oh, he's such a nice guy," Sid will reply with enthusiasm. "Well, that tells me nothing," Rosie will flash back. "Everyone you know is a nice guy."

Sid's first marriage was like a house built on a cliff-top, glorious for a while; the occasional stiff breeze but mostly the perfect place to sit out in the sun with a glass of red wine, a wheel of brie and a fresh-baked baguette. But sometimes cliffs erode and fall away, and there's nothing you can do about it except watch the rocks tumble and gradually accept one day your foundations will be rubble on the beach below. Sid did what he could; tried to be kind, soaked up the rage and contempt that dive-bombed and screeched round his head like territorial seagulls, went along to counselling to be told the many ways he'd got everything wrong, and paid the bills. Watching the ground beneath what had been his home drop in disintegrating lumps from right underneath them, he acknowledged the time had really come to move out at last.

Sid was the one who cleared up the mess at the end. He took thirty years of married life in thirty trips to the landfill site, though he hung onto some treasured photographs of the days they laughed together, young and brown in the sun at the water's edge – badly faded now, but precious nonetheless, to him.

Still, "Love wins," he said.

Doggedly, with everyone blaming him and no pains spared to inform the world of his shortcomings, Sid did the only thing he knew how to do – because he'd been doing it so long – he tried to be kind.

Sid believes in taking the long view. He knows you can reap nothing but what you sow.

With the passing of time, the bitterness and poisonous acridity of divorce began to subside. His children forgave him, and invited him to their weddings and then to his grandchildren's baptisms and birthday parties, to family Christmases and housewarmings. "Love wins," thought Sid, as he poured a generous glass of wine for his ex-wife, wooing back friendship where romance had been lost.

Sid knows that people forget, they move on, memories blur. He knows that if you are self-disciplined enough to refrain from spite and slander, forgiveness will grow like a weed in your garden. Hard words said about him, cruel things done to him – he lets them pass. This many years along the line, he and his ex-wife are friends, and his children's eyes reflect back the love they have always seen in his. "Love wins," says Sid – and it seems he's right.

This is not quite how Rosie sees life. She listens, she watches, and she takes note. She does not trust easily. She pulls up the drawbridge at the slightest sign of trouble – at no more than a cloud of dust on the far horizon that could as well be a friend as a foe.

Rosie's years have been devoted to the canny manufacture of ways and means. She knows how to renounce, how to move on, how to manage alone and on very little, how to hold still and breathe light when everything hurts too much. Rosie knows how to forage and scavenge. She can keep things together and find solutions. She does not blame, because what's the use of that? But she remembers. Her expectations of people are based on what they did before. "They let you down yesterday, they'll let you down tomorrow," says Rosie. She watches Sid and his patient loving, winning them over, buttoning his lip, taking the flak; and she wonders why he thinks it worth the while. "They're good people," says Sid, gently. "Are they?" Rosie questions. "You sure about that?"

And now, here they are, Rosie and her very small grandson, battle lines drawn. He stands just inside the front door of her house, stark naked, having torn off his clothes in a rage, roaring with the full power of his lungs for his mummy while tears pour down his flaming cheeks. He would leave right now, run into the street, but the handle is too high up for him to reach. He is just a little boy. Even so, his body shakes with ire, distraught, and the wet eyes of his flung back head are full of despair. Rosie, silent, gathers the toys into black bin liners, then stands with her arms folded, jaw tight, mouth sealed in a bloodless line, watching him.

Rosie never gives in. Nothing in all life has thrown at her has beaten her yet. She clings on to nothing – certainly not people – and she parries the adversary in any confrontation, implacably. Rosie avoids arguments when she can because she doesn't enjoy them; but she has never lost one.

She turns her back on the screaming child.

Being a grandmother is not how she thought. Her daughter is an analytical liberal; she informs herself and she thinks things through. She knows shame is toxic and humiliation is counter-productive. She knows you grow strong adults by being kind and patient with tempestuous toddlers; she knows love wins. She would gather up this storm-tossed child and soothe him. She would never have taken his toys. And she would never, whatever the circumstance, do what Rosie's hand itches to do now – administer a smart slap and then frogmarch the child up to his room. Rosie's daughter, like Sid, believes love wins. Rosie believes Rosie wins. Even so, she who is a watcher has observed how her daughter and Sid plan their campaigns, and she grasps the point about winning a battle but losing a war. Momentarily nonplussed, she wonders what to do next.

She deposits the bags of confiscated toys in the cupboard under the stairs – she will never give them back; Rosie's word can be depended on – then she walks quietly into the kitchen. She makes up a tray with a glass of apple juice – a glass, not a child's plastic cup, because he likes to do things the grown-up way – and a plate of chocolate chip cookies, his favourites. She takes the tray through to the family room, and sets it down on his little table, then goes back to where he stands, still shaky, crying hopelessly. He looks up at her, miserable, relying on her to find a way forward for them both. This she can do. People have been relying on Rosie to make things work her whole adult life. She looks back at him, weighing the situation. No future in asking him to put his clothes on just yet, that will only antagonize.

"Would you like a story?" she asks, straightforwardly. Her voice does not wheedle, or try to curry favour with this child. Slowly, he nods. She holds out her hand: "Come on then," she says.

Wrapped in a soft blanket, he sits beside her on the sofa, his body shaken by the occasional juddering sighs of ebbing trauma, nibbling his cookies, drinking carefully from the grown-up glass, spilling nothing. Red Riding Hood. Jack and the Beanstalk. The Wolf and the Seven Little Pigs. The ones he likes best.

Casually, as she puts the last book down, she asks him: "Would you like to get dressed ready for Mummy?" Eagerly, he complies.

"Granny threw my toys away," he tells his mother, later, his voice quavering with the ghosts of tragedy. His mother glances at her mother, enquiring. "That's right," says Rosie. "He won't pick them up; well then, I won't keep them here."

"He usually will if we do it together," her daughter comments, in that gentle way she has, as she helps him on with his shoes. But they don't argue.

Later, alone with a cup of tea, her feet up on the sofa, Rosie's thoughts drift. She regrets the meltdown. She feels foolish and inadequate that she can't handle this child better than she does. Somewhere deep, in a place she feels reluctant to open and examine, she knows that fighting accomplishes nothing. It's what Sid says. Love wins.

For sharing and wondering

- What were your favourite stories when you were little?
- What are the best ways to teach small children discipline and boundaries?
- Which aspects of your home life would you specially welcome God's help with at the moment?

Into the Mystery

Jesus, Friend of little children,
Be a friend to me;
Take my hand, and ever keep me
Close to Thee.

Teach me how to grow in goodness,
Daily as I grow;
Thou hast been a child, and surely
Thou dost know.

Never leave me, nor forsake me;
Ever be my friend;
For I need Thee, from life's dawning
To its end.

Walter J. Mathams (1853–1931)

7

Epiphany

"Three wise men following a star," says Rosie. "What's with that?"

"How do you mean?" Sid looks up from his sudoku puzzle, glances at the fire, picks up another log and pushes it carefully into the glowing pile.

"Well, it doesn't make sense."

"Because?"

"I've been to loads of different types of churches, Sid, and they all disagree with each other about almost everything. They all think the others have got it wrong. But if there's one thing they all do agree on, it's that astrology is twaddle. That's the mild version. Some of them think astrology is demonic. None of them have any respect for it at all. Yet here they are, every Christmas, telling the story of the Magi following the star. They saw it in the east, and they knew what it meant – that the king of all humanity, the god-king, had been born; and they came to worship him. Now then, if you started with just you and the Bible, no preconceptions, I'd say you'd conclude from reading this story that astrology is a very useful means of finding out what's going on. Where's the twaddle? Where's the evil? For heaven's sake – it led them to Jesus! Surely, if astrology lives up to the bad press the church gives it, either the men weren't wise or they weren't following the star."

Sid smiles at Rosie's indignation as she warms to her subject.

"I haven't been to the same churches as you," he says. "In the

Catholic church I never heard them talk about astrology at all, for good or bad. Nor in the Quakers. They don't even think about it. But, from the snippets I've picked up here and there, I'd say the general line is that, after they found Jesus, the wise men stopped following stars and followed him instead. When Matthew, telling the story, says 'they went home by another way', I think that might be way with a capital W. Their feet were on a different path after they met him. Matthew was writing in Syria, and looking at his Gospel it seems like he had a mixed bag of Jews and Gentiles in his congregation – and the Gentiles were Zoroastrian, which is what the Magi were. If you read his gospel carefully, you can see how he affirms both Judaism and Zoroastrianism, but redirects both of them into what he understands to be their fulfilment – a new and living way."

Rosie chews her lip, thinking hard about this.

"*But,*" she counters, "just as Matthew speaks with respect of the Law and the prophets – the Jewish guide to holiness – as fulfilled in the life of Jesus, so he's also respectful of astrology, the Zoroastrian way of exploring meaning. There's nothing in the way he portrays it to suggest it's either nonsense or wrong – just kind of incomplete. It's only a journey, but it's going in the right direction, surely, if the destination is Jesus."

"Well…" Sid turns over her words, considering. "I guess the objection people have to astrology is the idea of the stars controlling our destiny – affecting our lives. Where, if we are in God's hands, the outcomes rest with him."

Rosie snorts in derision. "Whoever thinks that knows nothing about astrology!" she exclaims. "The stars don't control our lives, and no astrologer ever said they did! The point of the astrological system is that all things are connected. The wise men didn't think Jesus appeared *because of the star* – they thought the star appeared because of Jesus. The meaning comes from him, not from the star, but because all things are woven together in the spiritual fabric of the cosmos, his coming will reverberate through the whole thing, so if you understand how to read it you will know. How could the Earth not respond to its creator come to dwell with us? How could his birth not be written in the stars? It's even in the psalms, about the heavens telling the glory of God, and night unto night revealing knowledge."[8]

Sid nods. Yes. It does say that in the psalms.

"But Jesus," Rosie carries on, "he's at the heart of life like the aniseed in the middle of a gobstopper, flavouring the whole thing. Time, life, events, gather round him, drawing their meaning from him. Everything he touches turns portentous! You know that thing in Isaiah about God's suffering servant – he was despised and rejected, but by his wounds we are healed?"[9]

"'Surely he hath borne our griefs and carried our sorrows,'"[10] murmurs Sid. "Yes, I know it."

"Well, people argue about whether it refers to Israel and is meant for the time it was written but just uncannily applies to Jesus, or if it was an actual foretelling about Jesus. But what if it's neither? What if it's about the way things always are, and the truth of how goodness is received by the world – what if it's just *life*; and because Jesus *is* the way, the truth and the life, it has to be about him?"

Sid looks at her. "I never thought of it like that," he says, intrigued.

"When I look at the life of Jesus," Rosie goes on, encouraged by his interest, "I see ordinary things flowering into their inherent meaning because of his presence. Like when he was born. He emerged from Mary's womb, and she would have received him into her hands and washed the blood of birth from his body; his body, his blood. And it's a prefiguring; when he died, she received his body, and washed the blood of death from him, and laid him into the tomb – the Earth's womb; gave his life back to God. It balances. And then the resurrection opens it out into an endless cycle of life

8 Psalm 19.
9 Isaiah 53:3–5.
10 Isaiah 53:4.

– his body, his blood, his real presence with us. It's Eucharistic, and the Eucharist takes simple, everyday food – bread and wine – and draws out their meaning, body and blood, the presence of Christ. Bread which is life, life-giving, and wine for death, spilt blood. Wine *will* kill you too, if you drink enough of it. Wine is dangerous. Life is dangerous. That's how it is."

"Rosie," says Sid, "I'm glad I married you. Would you like a glass of very dangerous wine?"

She laughs. "Yes, please. I would."

He opens the bottle, pours it, offers her the glass. They sit in silence by the fire. Sid holds his glass so the firelight glows through it, revealing its hidden depths.

"Stars, wine, bread…" he says. "Light, birth, death… Jesus at the midst of it all. Life is holy, Rosie."

For sharing and wondering

- What are your thoughts on astrology, and how have you reached those views?
- Matthew's church community had to work on creating harmony between Jews and Zoroastrians. What different groups can you identify in your church, and is their relationship harmonious or could it do with some re-balancing?
- Think of a social group towards whom you know your attitude is prejudiced, and for whom you would like God's help to be more understanding.

Into the Mystery

You called the stars into being, O God, and you ordered their courses in the heavens. Our lives are but a speck of dust in a sunbeam in this great cosmos your word has ordained. May our understanding of the nature of life make space for the infinite possibility of your magnificence, as well as the homely detail of your kindness, grace and love.

8

Candlemas/Imbolc/St Brigid

Sid grew up a Catholic and ended up a Quaker. As a child he went to Mass with his mother in a most beautiful church, a high holy space of pale stone; its architecture modern, simple, spare, columns rising and morning light pouring in through the windows, incense smoke drifting through the sunbeams.

Curious about monasticism, at the end of his teens he went to find the Benedictine monks in the abbey near the university where he studied. He sat in the shadows of their cavernous chapel, listening to the quiet ebb and flow of their voices in the Compline chants, and loved it absolutely. The silences, the spaces, the ineffable peace.

Later he read more widely, about religious persecutions and inquisitions, and much of the shine came off his Christian faith – he had no taste for schism or homophobia or tribalism. The rift between Catholic and Protestant felt like a pain to him, like a dangerous fault-line in his world.

At church youth services he had come across the songs and prayers from the community at Iona, which made him curious about Celtic Christianity. He began to explore the Celtic roots of his faith, the old paths and patterns of the days before Roman Catholicism overran the British Isles. As he read about the monastic missionaries who came across the sea from Ireland to Scotland and England bringing the gospel to their pagan peoples, he traced something earthy and vivid, imaginative and eminently natural in what they had put in place.

The ancient (pagan) Celts believed in the divine Mystery; the realm of Weird, something around and beyond, something that touched upon them but was always elusive, entered by most people only at the door of death but breaking in here and there in the thin places. On their small farms, sensitive to the numinous qualities of light and dark and dependent on the harvests and the health of beasts, they marked the round of the year with Fire Festivals, celebrations of life's sacred mysteries – fertility, beginnings and endings, sharing and cleansing, memory, story, love, home, the natural world, the cycle of birth and death. At the summer and winter solstices, at the spring and autumn equinoxes, they marked the turning of the year in their quarter days. Then they bisected the times between by fire festivals on the cross-quarter days, and so made a reverential wheel of the agricultural year, scrying into the mystery of life, making remembrance of meaning underlying routine events, observing the holy in the ordinary.

When the monks came across the sea from Ireland, they proved gentle missionaries of the gospel, respectful of the ancient ways and tactful in their evangelization. They also believed in the holiness of what is natural. They too saw the glimmers of divine mystery in the sparkle of sunlight on the sea. They knew about angels, about the worship that arises to God from creation – the endless chant of praise, the deep, slow bass note of rock and hill, of 100-year oak trees, the glorious soprano of skylark, nightingale and wren. They understood that the world is alive.

So, instead of displacing the ancient rhythm of sacred observance, they built the Christian story into it. Alongside the Celtic holy days they placed their saints' days, the feasts and fasts of the church – and that was how they told the story of the gospel, and taught the pagan people to love it.

Imbolc, the first of the four fire festivals (the cross-quarter days) falls halfway between the winter solstice and the spring equinox at the beginning of February. Celebrating the passing of winter and the first shoots of spring, the changing of the goddess from the crone to the maiden, it honours the birth of the sun and marks the recovery of the goddess after giving birth to the god. It was customary to light a candle in every room of the house, even if only briefly, on this festival. It is a time of cleansing – a time to turn out the house, sweep everything, shake everything, start afresh. The Earth is waking up.

Alongside Imbolc, the missionary monks set the feast of Candlemas and St Brigid's Day. Candlemas marks the purification of the Blessed Virgin Mary after the birth of Christ. So in their peaceable liturgical commentary, the monks worked with the pagan year, making connections with the gospel, beginning to weave the new ways in with the old. They did not confront, they blended. They helped the people see that Christ is at the heart of creation, was there from the beginning, hates nothing but illumines and transforms everything.

Sid finds profound satisfaction in this way of going about things – natural, gentle, seeing into what is already there and finding the links of truth. He believes that every religion has its insights and contributions to make – its offerings for the altar of the one, true, living God. When he thinks of the coming of Roman Catholicism to the British Isles, deposing the earthy and simple Christianity of the Celts, supplanting it with the hierarchies and canon law modelled on the civilization of the Roman empire, a sense of mourning wells up inside him. He prefers the fires and the thin places, the sweeping of the hearth and the veneration of wells and springs as the womb-opening of earth, to the men on thrones in their tall pointy hats and their subjugation of women. Sid likes equality, and acceptance. He sees more of God in the cautious fox and the rising sun, the lifted head of the deer and the spilling riot of a rambling rose, than he does in the Holy Roman Pontiff waving from his balcony. Thinking about it, Sid's exodus from Roman Catholicism was sooner or later inevitable.

Today, the 1st February, is St Brigid's Day. Sid brings a candle to the breakfast table. The pale sun of early spring will soon be risen. He eats his porridge slowly, as the shadows of dawn lighten and night recedes. He thinks about St Brigid – simple and humble, generous and pure, lover of art and beauty and worker of miracles. He thinks about Candlemas, on the 2nd February, tomorrow. He imagines candles shining in every separate home in those farm dwellings of the Dark Ages. The Celtic day begins at dusk, not dawn – so both St Brigid's Day today and Candlemas tomorrow fall on the feast of Imbolc. Those canny Irish monks got two for the price of one. Sid smiles at their divine economy. They were no fools, he thinks. Stories are the way to go, not antagonism. His mind wanders to the book he was reading at bedtime last night, and a remembered phrase: "You will never change anybody by shouting at them."[11] Too true, thinks Sid.

He leans forward and cups the candle flame with his hand, blows it out. But he leaves the candle there. He will light it at every mealtime on this special day that welcomes the birth of the year's light and speaks of purity.

He pushes back the bench he's sitting on, taking his porridge bowl to the sink, washing it and leaving it to drain on the board. He sets the kettle to boil.

The sun is risen now. Sid takes a hot cup of tea upstairs to Rosie, who is just beginning to stir.

For sharing and wondering

- What have been the strongest influences on your faith?
- In what circumstances do you find it easiest to pray quietly, or to worship with others?
- If you were to make a home-based ceremony for celebrating the start of spring, what would you include?

11   The title of a chapter in Alexander McCall Smith's *The Double Comfort Safari Club*.

Into the Mystery

Your love, O Lord, shapes the seasons of our lives and the rhythms of the turning world. Help us to be sensitive and appreciative to your wisdom and grace in whatever is happening just now in our lives. Help us to discern your hand at work, and to be faithful in joining in the endeavour and creativity of your love.

9

Ash Wednesday

"Are you going to the Ash Wednesday service, Rosie?"

"The imposition of ashes? No."

"Oh dear. That sounds very decided. Why not?"

Rosie dips in and out of church attendance anyway. Sometimes she goes, sometimes not. Usually that depends on how she's feeling and what she can face. Human society is sometimes too much for her. But Sid thinks this sounds like something more than just how things are with Rosie today.

"I don't like what they say," Rosie answers him. A bit cryptic for Sid. "Explain?" he prompts.

"They put the ashes on your forehead, and they say to you: 'Remember that dust you are, and to dust you shall return.'[12] I don't like it. It's like a curse. Where it comes from in the book of Genesis is the creation of Adam. His name is a pun – it's a masculine form from the Hebrew word *adamah*, which means 'earth'. So his name is really 'Earthy' or 'Earthling'. And it's because God made him from the dust of the Earth. Adam was made from the Earth, so he bears her name. It's like being someone's child: your dad was called George Ashley, and you – Sid Ashley – bear his name because you came from him, you are his child. Adam is 'Earthy' because he comes from the Earth. But the Earth is a living being, the Earth is vibrant and teems with life. To be the child of Earth is not the same as to be the child of dust.

12 Drawn from Genesis 3:19.

We are made of Earth's substance, and are thereby connected with all of creation. Earth has her home in us because we are made of Earth. And for that same reason, we have our home in her. It's like the Buddhists would put it: 'I take refuge in the Earth, and the Earth takes refuge in me.' The whole of Earth, not only the dust.

"But anyway, that was no more than the first part of the story. When God made Adam from the dust of the Earth, Adam was just a lifeless form until God breathed his Spirit into him. Just a little puff, the Bible story says. And it was that little puff of the breath of God – God's living Spirit – that changed Adam from a lifeless form to a *nephesh* – a living being. A human being – and if we have a point at all, this is it – is a fusion of the substance of the Earth and the breath of God (his Spirit). We are at home in two worlds. We are spiritual as much as we are physical. We have a heavenly father and our mother is the Earth. That's why Jesus, incarnating the divine, is not an oddity, a one-off hybrid; he fulfils our nature, our destiny, what we were created to be.

"Now this imposition of ashes kind of negates all of that. It's like an insult, like a slap in the face. It ignores the whole beautiful drawing into life of what a human being is, the intimate infusion of the breath of God into the stuff of the living Earth. It takes something burnt, dead – ashes. It picks up on the 'dust' half of 'dust of the Earth' and ignores completely the 'Earth' half, and doesn't even acknowledge the breath of God, without which we are not beings by any definition. It makes out that we are death-stuff. But we're not. 'The glory of God is a human being fully alive.'[13] To say we are dust is reductionist to the point of becoming untrue.

"I could accept 'Of the Earth you were made and to the Earth you will one day return.' There is peace in that for me. I know that nothing lasts for ever, that everything born will also one day die. I see my body ageing and changing. I see the spring blossoms burgeon

13 Quotation from St Irenaeus. Actually he said, "The glory of God is a living man" or "The glory of God is a man alive" – and perhaps that may refer to Jesus, or to the resurrection. But it is legitimate to invoke it as Rosie does here.

into summer fruit, and fall from the tree in autumn – ripening, then rotting, and becoming once more part of the Earth from which they grew. The flower grows from the compost, but the compost in turn is made from the flower. That's the cycle of life, and I am at peace with that.

"But it's also true that the Spirit in me witnesses with the Spirit of God. In Jesus I enter the wonder of eternal life, and I will not deny that, or have it gainsaid. Spirit I am, and to Spirit I will return. That is my certain hope, and any words spoken over me that do not include or acknowledge that are so incomplete as to be profoundly inaccurate.

"So, no. I don't have anything to do with the imposition of ashes."

Sid can see his wife has thought this through in some detail. Even so, he ventures to say: "I think what it's meant to be is a call to humility. A reminder of our lowliness. It's part of the penitential aspect of being a Christian. Like a reverential prostration before the altar of the living God – an admission that before him we are nothing, that faced with his glory we see that we are mere specks of dust. It is, in its way, an expression of awe."

Rosie looks at him. "But, that's the thing, Sid. Before God I am exactly not 'nothing'. It is in coming before God that I find meaning, hope, grace – *life*. Faced with his glory, light infuses my whole being, enters me, illuminates me – enlightens me. In the presence of God I am a spark, not a speck of dust. I find my Buddha-nature, my Christ-light, my true self, when I come before his throne. Awe, yes. But also wonder. A human being fully alive."

"Fair enough." Sid knows when he is beaten. After all, he wasn't going to the service either. Even so, he sees something beautiful in the kneeling, in the humility, in accepting – embracing, even – that death is actually a part of life, has a place in our nature *because* we are alive. But he doesn't want to get into an argument about it.

52

For sharing and wondering

- How do you, or your church community, observe Lent?
- How do you respond to the words "Remember that dust you are and to dust you shall return"?
- What place does confession or penance have in your own life?

Into the Mystery

The beautiful Earth was brought into being by the breath of your Spirit, Creator God, and humanity is the creature of stardust, living earth, breath made manifest. May we ever rejoice in the holy origins of our life, for we are fearfully and wonderfully made.

10

Lent 1 – Wabibito

"Wabibito."

That's what someone – Rosie, presumably – has scrawled on the back of the envelope lying on the kitchen table. Sid props it up against the box of granola and looks at it as he chews his breakfast.

Wabibito. What the heck is that?

Rosie comes in from the garden. She's been hanging out the washing, making the most of this breezy day – the first with a clear sky, and no ominous clouds gathering, for a long time. The gust of air that whooshes in with her is bracing. It's spring, but only just. Very Lenten.

"Wabibito." Sid looks up at her, questioningly, as she stashes the laundry basket in its corner and puts the tub of clothes pegs back on the shelf under the window. "What is it?"

She grins at him. "Three guesses. Here's your first clue. It's Japanese."

"It's the name of a sushi restaurant!"

"Wrong. It's not a place or a kind of food."

"Um… clothes, then – a scarf? A hat? The sash for a kimono?"

He keeps trying as she shakes her head, teasing. "Stop, Sid, stop! It's not a garment. Here's another clue. It's a kind of person."

"A baby! Like the Italian 'bambino'!"

"Wrong, wrong, all completely wrong. Shall I tell you, then?"

She takes her favourite mug, the work of a local potter, from its hook under the shelves of crockery fixed to the wall above the sink, and pours herself a cup of tea from the big pot Sid has set to brew on the table.

"Well," she says, "you know the Japanese term *'wabi-sabi'*?"

"Yes," says Sid; then, "No. I mean, I've heard it but I'm not quite sure… It's something like 'shabby chic', isn't it? Some type of aesthetic, style – that sort of thing?"

"Wabi-sabi," says Rosie, tipping a small pile of granola on to the table to nibble with her cup of tea, "is a composite of two quite separate Japanese words. 'Sabi' is a term for the beauty of something old – like much-handled tools or well-used furniture; even an old person. The comfortable smoothness, the serenity – a velveteen rabbit kind of thing.[14] Autumn leaves, a mended pot, a patched coat, a darned sock. I guess it arises from a Buddhist mindset, with that focus on transience, impermanence; this too shall pass, death-in-life. 'Sabi' can even mean simply 'rust', which gives you an idea of what it's all about – the loveliness of a lichened wall, a mossy stone.

"The other word, 'wabi', denotes a loneliness, a melancholy – someone alone in nature. Like Jesus in the wilderness. Something chill or lean or withered, something unwanted. You know that aria from the *Messiah* – 'He was despised, rejected, a man of sorrows and acquainted with grief'?[15] That's quite wabi.

"Then around the fourteenth century, the meaning of wabi began to change, taking on connotations of quietness and lowliness, the beauty of humble objects, rustic simplicity – the subtle and understated elegance of natural or handmade things. I mean, quite crude things, even broken and mended, rough-hewn.

"The words were taken up and coupled together into the aesthetic quest for beauty in Japan, and 'wabi-sabi' is how the language put its finger on the particular quality of unpretentious and humble

14 *The Velveteen Rabbit (or How Toys Become Real)* is a classic children's story (first published 1922) by Margery Williams, illustrated by William Nicholson, about a stuffed toy's quest to become real. He achieves it through the love of the child to whom he belongs.
15 Isaiah 53:3.

simplicity, the natural loveliness of ordinary and earthy things – roughened and unconventional. And also, an association with wisdom in the life that follows plain humility."

Sid smiles. "Sounds very Quaker," he says.

"Yes!" Rosie nods enthusiastically. "And Shaker, too – though possibly a little less neat and tidy than the Shaker ideal. But that kind of thing. With a certain loneliness and detachment in there somewhere."

"And – 'wabibito'?"

"Well, a wabibito is a person whose life is characterized by wabi-sabi qualities. Someone humble and unpretentious, frugal and thoughtful and solitary. A person who works with their own hands and dresses in simple clothes. Someone content with very little, with what is ordinary and natural. Maybe an old man in a darned sweater drinking his tea from a cup that's had the handle broken and glued back on, sitting in his garden with his dog, the companion of many years, at his feet, wearing his friendly old hat and watching the wind blow dead leaves in eddies round his boots worn to the shape of his feet, his gait, over decades of wear. That's a wabibito."

Sid takes this in. "Sounds nice," he says. "Sounds peaceful and comfortable. Why did you write it down?"

"Well, I was listening to a Lent church service on the radio, and they had a reading from the Bible – it said something about how we should make it our ambition to live a quiet life and work with our own hands,[16] and then in the talk they referenced another Bible quotation I thought really lovely – it spoke of wanting all men everywhere to lift up holy hands in prayer without anger or argument.[17] And the speaker talked about Jesus sitting quietly alone in the desert, a place of wild beasts and angels, very earthy and very heavenly at the same time. The wisdom of prayer, and the ordinariness of bread and of stones. How Jesus took time to pray, and how he thought about bread, and took it into his hands and broke it. How he took a cup of

16 1 Thessalonians 4:11.
17 1 Timothy 2:8.

red wine into his hands, and it became holy because he was grateful – he gave thanks for it. And how our everyday lives can become something profound and beautiful if we learn a wise discipline of humility, giving thanks for what comes to our hands, content with having little, being little, with simplicity. All that kind of thing. I really enjoyed it. The man had a gentle voice, and he spoke slowly. And I thought, oh my gosh, Jesus was a wabibito. He was a wabi-sabi kind of person.

"All my life I've wanted to be a wabibito, Sid. To find the wisdom of simple things, and live close to the Earth. To be humble and modest and quiet, keeping a discipline of solitude. To accept change gracefully, learning to let go, relinquishing what has had its day. To understand that all things pass, and therefore each unique moment is utterly precious and at the same time doesn't matter very much. It's what I want."

"I see," says Sid. "And these wabibitos – some of them have your shopping habit?"

He's joking, but he watches her face fall and the eagerness drain away, and wishes he hadn't said it. It feels like a cheap shot, when he sees its effect.

"No," she says, and she sounds sad. "No, they don't. They would be satisfied with a little house in the wilderness, and a stone bowl set to catch the water channelled by a bamboo pipe from the spring. I don't think you see wabibitos in the high street."

"Well… eBay, maybe," Sid smiles at her, wanting to make amends, but knowing it's too late and cannot be done.

And then he sees something else. Although the moment is broken, because he was clumsy, even this also shall pass. It can be repaired with love and kindness, with the humility of being willing to understand and forgive. To get over things. All love that is real love is weathered with age and bears the scars of human clumsiness. Scars in its hands, in its feet. This, too, is wabi-sabi.

For sharing and wondering

- What are your favourite artefacts?
- What are the simple, humble things that make you happy?
- In what ways might you find it helpful to simplify your life?

Into the Mystery

In quietness and humility, O Lord, you came to share our lives. To an ordinary family, working with wood, walking in the hills. In the normal circumstances of daily life help us to find the wonder and blessing of your presence, for you are always with us.

11

Lent 2 – The Bell Curve

"I thought Quakers didn't observe Lent."

Every year, Sid gives up something for Lent. This time he's given up tea, which feels so hard to do – a real sacrifice. The first day was OK, but by the third day he had a raging headache. He's through that now, but still feels forlorn in the afternoons, in the 4 p.m. half-hour that should have had a cup of tea in it.

"They don't," he replies, feeling tetchy and making the effort to sound at least civil. "I guess it must be the residual Catholic in me. I'm trying to give that up too, but it seems to be here to stay."

"Some people say you should take up something for Lent as a change from giving up things," observes Rosie. "I suppose, depending on a person's temperament, taking something up could be way more penitential than giving up things. Maybe you could do both. Take up helping with the coffee rota after meeting, then give it up because it's so not fun."

"Yeah. Maybe giving up sarcasm for Lent could work for some people."

"Ouch. Oh dear. Sorry, Sid. Well, anyway – cup of coffee? Herb tea? What would you like? Dandelion? Peppermint? Liquorice? Fennel? Nettle? I've got them all here."

She turns in the silence and looks at Sid's despondent face. "Oh, Sid! For goodness' sake have a cup of tea if that's what you really want. Stuff Lent."

He shakes his head. No. You stick to what you started. "Some coffee would be nice. Thanks, Rosie."

"Giving things up," she says as she waits for the kettle to boil, "is a habit and an art and a skill. Well worth learning."

She gets out the mugs, and spoons the instant coffee granules into his – not too strong; he doesn't actually like instant coffee. She hesitates over hers and decides on herb tea. Making regular tea for herself right here, right now, might rub salt into the wound. She adds milk to his coffee, and gives him a cookie to go with it – this will make it more palatable for him, she knows. Sid will probably put on weight this Lent. Rosie's private opinion is that it would have been a shrewder move to stick with the tea and give up cookies, but she can see some thoughts are best kept to herself.

"We're taking this drink by the fire, yes?"

It's still cold out. They don't usually light the fire until the evening, but Rosie did today, to take the chill off the air. They carry their drinks through to sit in comfy chairs, and Rosie curls herself up, loving the fragrance of the wood burning.

"Relinquishment..." she says. "'We brought nothing into this world, and it is certain we can carry nothing out.' Who said that? Thomas Cranmer?[18] Is it from the Book of Common Prayer?[19] Is it in the Bible?"[20]

She looks at him questioningly, but Sid doesn't know.

"Whatever. It's true. Our relationship with the material plane goes like a bell curve. We start with nothing at all – not even hair or teeth. Our first challenge in life is acquisition. Food, warmth, strength, health... then skills, knowledge, friends... then a vocation – or at least an occupation – and income, possessions, a home, security, a mate, a family. Climbing the bell curve. It's necessary. It's the actual stuff of life. Acquiring.

"I'm not sure at what point we reach the top exactly, but sooner

18 No.
19 No.
20 Yes. 1 Timothy 6:7.

or later impermanence kicks in, and we start to come down the other side and have to give it all back. Our kids grow up and leave home, we retire from our work, our muscle strength declines, our memory starts to go, our hearing and eyesight fade, our hair and teeth fall out, our friends and family – the people we grew up with and travelled along with – start to die all around us. Then our health goes, our organs fail and it's the O Mega. Did you know that, Sid? That Omega – the last letter of the Greek alphabet – is an image of death? It's an arch, a big doorway. O Mega – the Big Zero. The end."

She sips her fennel tea, and contemplates the flames. Sid nods in affirmation about the Omega, but says nothing. He eats his cookie but it's not the same without tea. Roll on Easter. The next few weeks will be miserable. Why is tea so important to him? It's more than just a drink; it's comfort and familiarity and tradition. All his family, all his friends – everyone drinks tea. It's what you do together. It's so hard to give it up. He wishes now he'd picked chocolate or something else he doesn't care about. And he can't believe he even thought that; it makes him feel ashamed.

"So," says Rosie, " the smart thing to do is make relinquishment a skill you take trouble to learn. What it says in *Desiderata* – 'Surrender gracefully the things of youth.'[21] Buddhists teach about this. They are encouraged to contemplate the impermanence of life, and remember that all things pass; everything must change, nothing is forever.

"I think if you know this, life is sweeter, more vivid. If you live with the awareness that one day you will no longer have this – any of it. You will have to give it all back. It's odd – it makes it all matter less and yet you enjoy it more. Clutching and clinging and grabbing ruins life. Sitting lightly to it makes it more happy.

"Even the difficult things – divorce, illness, job redundancy, bereavement – they present practical problems, but you can meet them with some kind of equanimity if you knew all along you'd lose what you had one day. It helps you make peace with life.

21 1927 prose poem by US writer Max Ehrmann.

"I read about a hospice philosophy of making 'the best possible day' the target. Working with people experiencing broad and severe loss – well, dying – they look at what between them they can do, with medicine and the possibilities that remain, to make each day the best possible day.

"And maybe, whatever point you are on the bell curve, that would be the wise move. To know that this too shall pass, and to make of it the best possible day."

Sid feels this wave of incredible sadness as he listens to her. He has lived through so much loss in his lifetime. He has been so lonely. Silly, he knows it, but somehow he had it in mind that this would be forever – their love, their old house and its green garden, the cat and the fireside, the changing seasons and the countryside. But of course… you just have to let it go.

"And the best possible day," says Rosie, "isn't going to be something that just randomly happens to you – though spontaneity and wonderful surprises can be brilliant. It's something you have to bring about yourself."

"With help from other people, and from God," Sid points out.

"Of course. But they can't do it all for you, even so. In the end it's your call for it to be the best possible day or not. It's what you make of it. Some people, you could give them the moon and they'd still want it in another colour."

They have finished their drinks.

"Fire's dying down Sid. We've both got work to do. Shall I let it go out now?"

For sharing and wondering

- What do you like to take on extra, or give up, for Lent?
- Think of a time in your life when you were unexpectedly required to let go of someone or something. What happened?
- What wise habits of mind and life might you think of putting in place, to prepare for your old age?

Into the Mystery

You are God, even to the uttermost. From before we are born, through whatever life brings, into our old age, you watch over us, and you are there with us when we die. To our living, to our dying, to what we do and have, and to what we relinquish, bring the peace of your presence we pray, Lord of all our beginnings and our endings.

12

Lent 3 – Love Vast as the Ocean

Rosie drifts from church to church like a tumbleweed; a feral and lonely wandering, searching for a way in from a self-imposed exile of her own making. The structures alienate and oppress her – competitive spirituality ("the one true church") doesn't mean anything to her. Life emanates from Mystery – that she knows – but not one that can be formulated into a creed or hemmed in by thirty-nine articles of religion. She cannot make sense out of something that would attempt to express the nature of God in such terms.

But still she likes to listen to the morning service on the radio. It allows her to consider the thought processes of the church militant here on Earth from a safe distance. And today they sing a hymn that catches her attention.

"Here is love, Sid. Vast as the ocean, it said![22] And loving-kindness as a flood. But… oh, Sid. I cannot avail myself of it."

This is not really Quaker-speak. This vocabulary brings Sid to the shores of evangelical Christianity, of which he is profoundly suspicious. He will have to go cautiously here. It sounds as though Rosie is in one of her Dark Nights, and what she says next proves him right, waving her hands vaguely in the air like something trapped in a veil he can't see.

22 "Here is love, vast as the ocean". Words by William Rees 1802–83.

"Like the night wind blowing in the dark, we come from nothing and we go to nothing. Dust we are, and to dust we shall return.[23] Even though it is stardust, it is only dust. Drifting in space. Love vast as the ocean! How lovely that sounds! A net flung wide enough, spun fine enough, to catch even a mote of dust. Ooh… wait a minute… that's what it says in the *Tao Te Ching*, isn't it? 'Heaven's net is spread wide, and even though the mesh is coarse, nothing slips through.'[24] But is it true, Sid? Or are we just falling?"

Sid is beginning to feel bemused. The flip-flop between evangelicalism and Taoism is leaving him behind. But he has a go, because her eyes are fixed on him now, and they contain a plea he cannot refuse. "Nothing," he says. "Yes. No-thing. We are not things and we are not born of a thing. We are being, and we come from life. I AM. We are dust, falling through light, but… remember that photo we saw, Rosie? The NASA photo of Earth as a miniscule pale blue dot somewhere in the shaft of a sunbeam? All Earth's moments are like that. Just a heartbreaking breath, the smallest event, no bigger than the point of a pin, but – crucially – caught and held in the light. By the light we are seen, and its streaming is our being.

"It seems to me that anyone who glimpses the paradox of life, its vast immensity like arches beyond arches rising into shadow, into the cathedral of the sky – and its contrasting frailty and insignificance, dust in the sunbeam – is bound to have their mind a little blown. You can dodge and twist and try to scurry away from that existential world of the massive and the tiny with all its terror and vertigo, but only by taking shelter in illusion.

"Did you ever read *The Screwtape Letters*, Rosie?"

"What?" She looks at him abstractedly. "No."

"It's by C. S. Lewis – you should read it, it's a great book. Funny and wise and full of truth. It's about a junior devil tasked with the corruption of a human soul, corresponding with his satanic line

23 If you think that's not what she said on Ash Wednesday, well Sid agrees with you. People are like that.
24 Tao Te Ching, Lao Tsu, chapter 73.

manager. There's a bit in it where the senior devil advises him on the best way to keep the human's mind from dwelling upon mystery and stumbling into truth. He says that because human nature is physical – the dust in the sunbeam thing – as well as spiritual, the trick is to draw the mind's attention to the continual flow of sensory experience, calling it real life and not for a moment allowing the mind to pause and consider what might be meant by 'real'. The advanced devil in the story reminisces about the occasion when a soul he was successfully drawing down to damnation sat in the library reading a book that began to awaken his mind to wonder. Hastily, the devil put the thought in his head that it was time for lunch, countering the idea that this was more important than lunch with the notion that it was precisely too important to try and tackle at the end of the morning. As the man heads off out of the library in search of a restaurant, the devil calls his attention to the newsboy on the corner and the No 73 bus going by, and convinces him that this – not the wonder of mystery beginning to flower in his mind in the library – is 'real life'. You should read that book, Rosie; I've got it in my study. You'd like it, I think."

"The devil?" she says. "Damnation? You believe all that?"

Sid suppresses a sigh. "Rosie… I'm a Quaker. We don't see life in those terms. Though I must say, I do see Mammon at large. I do see the world going to hell in a handbasket when I look at what a fast food chain can do to a rainforest. But that's something else.

"All I wanted to say is, when you look at life's immensity and your own littleness, such fragile being, it's bound to be terrifying. But, isn't that the 'vast as the ocean' part of the love? Even if we are falling dust, transient and ephemeral, our lives no more than a breath, isn't it a thing of wonder to be caught for this living moment in the light of a sunbeam? Worth the terror, maybe. *And* – even if we are no more than a breath, still, consider whose breath it is! Creatures of fusion, the dust of the Earth and the breath of the living God. It's all wonder, all mystery. Well, not quite all. It's also love. I do believe that."

Sid watches her face, the bewilderment and perplexity shifting and digging itself in. He gets up, and crosses the room to her, takes her in his arms. As she lays her head against his shoulder, feeling the softness of his sweater against her cheek, feeling his warmth and the infinite comfort of his embrace, his kindness, she asks him: "Isn't this the distraction that devil wrote about? C. S. Lewis, I mean. Isn't this the delusion of 'real life' that will drag my soul down to damnation? Your cardigan, our kitchen, a hug?"

"No, sweetheart," says Sid, always patient. "This is the love."

For sharing and wondering

- What helps you feel close to God?
- What are your beliefs about the devil?
- At times when you feel lonely and alienated, small and afraid, what comforts you?

Into the Mystery

Here is love, vast as the ocean,
Lovingkindness as the flood,
When the Prince of Life, our Ransom,
Shed for us His precious blood.
Who His love will not remember?
Who can cease to sing His praise?
He can never be forgotten,
Throughout Heav'n's eternal days.

On the mount of crucifixion,
Fountains opened deep and wide;
Through the floodgates of God's mercy
Flowed a vast and gracious tide.
Grace and love, like mighty rivers,
Poured incessant from above,
And Heav'n's peace and perfect justice
Kissed a guilty world in love.

William Rees (1802-83)

13

Lent 4 – Mothering Sunday

"Sid," says Rosie, "do you know how Mothering Sunday began? I thought it was named for the tradition of girls in domestic service having a day off to go and see their mothers. But I read the other day that it's not about real mothers at all – they went back to their mother church. Which is it?"

"Both," says Sid. "Just a minute."

He's making an unrealistically complicated cheesecake. It requires crème pâtissière, dissolved gelatin, beaten egg yolks with sugar, beaten egg white with sugar (but not as much as meringue), cream cheese, squeezed lemons and grated lemon rind. Every time he starts this, Sid remembers why he hardly ever makes it. He has the bain-marie on the hotplate gently heating the milk for the crème pâtissière, and another saucepan heating water for his gelatin. Managing the beaters is a challenge because they have to be entirely dry and free of grease to whisk the egg whites, but he needs them to whisk the crème pâtissière first, which has grease in it from the egg yolks and milk – and after he's washed them up it's so hard to get them properly dry in all the intersections of the metal bits. He has to cut out greaseproof paper shapes to line his tin, and crush some digestive biscuits then combine them with melted butter for the base. The butter is melting now on the third hotplate, and he has to keep an eye on it to be sure it melts completely but doesn't begin to brown. He knows the cheesecake will be delicious, but is it worth the hassle? Every bowl and pan he has is pressed into service, every counter top is covered with things. Sid is beginning to feel stressed.

"Laetare Sunday," he says, carefully stirring the gelatin to be sure it's completely dissolved, "takes its name from the introit set for the Mass on that day – *Laetare, Jerusalem*. It means, 'O be joyful, Jerusalem'. The introit's longer than that, obviously. Those are just the first two words. Ouch!" (He's burned his finger.)

Sid takes the butter off the heat and runs the cold water tap over the burn on his finger for a few moments. "The people of God look to Jerusalem as their mother. And it's called 'Rose Sunday' for the vestments worn on that day. The rose is a feminine emblem. So the custom grew up…" He slides the digestive biscuits into a plastic supermarket carrier bag, and bashes them vigorously with the rolling pin he fishes out of the drawer, to reduce them to crumbs. "… of people going back to their mother church to worship on that day – like the ancient Hebrews going up Mount Zion to worship at the temple. It followed that if you went back to your mother church – your home church, the one you went to before you took your job as a scullery maid or whatever – that your family would be there, so you would scoop the collateral benefit of visiting with your mother. Mothering Sunday – take your pick: your own actual mother, the church, Jerusalem. Mind you…" He's lined the tin, greased the paper, pressed down the biscuit mix into it, grated the lemon rind and squeezed the juice. He's working on the crème pâtissière now. "… maybe those are not separate. Perhaps they're a kind of amalgam of one idea. Motherness. Maternity. Whatever the right word is."

He takes the crème pâtissière off the heat, and there's that thoughtful, timeless moment when he tastes it – pauses to consider – yes, it's OK. At least this cheesecake is lemon, so he hasn't had to faff about slicing a vanilla pod in two along its length.

"How strange," says Rosie.

"What?" Sid looks round at his chaos of implements and ingredients, slightly alarmed. "What's strange?"

But Rosie isn't thinking about cheesecake. "I didn't get on with my mother very well. I mean she was a nice enough woman but I think we came from two different planets. She never really knew me and I knew her all too well. And I have a very uneasy relationship with the church; I'm not a big fan, to be honest. And Jerusalem… well, when I think of the Holy Land with its incessant violence and apartheid, what's to like? And as for being a mother – I was never a very good one. Tired, depressed and anxious, never knowing how to make ends meet. I wasn't much fun as a mother. Mother's Day is made into such a big deal nowadays. Makes me want to run and hide."

Sid has whisked his egg whites to perfection, and gets the crème pâtissière out of the freezer – he knows he shouldn't put a pan of hot sauce in the freezer, but he wants it cold, in short order. He sticks his finger in it experimentally. Yes, almost cool enough. He begins to tidy up his culinary debris, tossing things into the sink.

"Dame Julian of Norwich said Jesus is our true mother," he says. "She said God is both our father and our mother. Might that help? Or might you think of mothering in terms of its archetypal dimension? Nurturing, feeding, loving, bringing something to birth, taking care of something or someone? If you think of a cow licking her newborn calf so tenderly, or a hen gathering her brood under the shelter of her wings? Might Mothering Sunday be the day to celebrate especially that aspect of life, of God, of people? Birth Sunday. Tenderness Sunday. Nurturing Sunday. You could celebrate it," he says, "very appropriately – because the cow is the ultimate mother and her milk nourishes all of us; well, apart from vegans and lactose-intolerants I suppose – with a large slice of my glorious lemon cheesecake. Ta da!"

"Sid…" Rosie has no words for the unbelievable deliciousness of this cheesecake. No words. It takes heavenly scrumptiousness up to the next level.

"Where did you get this recipe?"[25] she says eventually.

Sid grins at her. "Where do you think? From my mother."

For sharing and wondering

- What is your favourite dessert?
- What is/was your relationship with your mother like?
- How do you find it helpful to think of God? As a father? As a mother? As a friend? Or… ?

Into the Mystery

Loving God, we thank you for all those who have mothered us – men or women, our birth mothers or not. Thank you for kindness and nurturing, for comfort and strength that have flowed into our lives from the love of our fellow human beings.

---

25 In case you want to have a go at Sid's lemon cheesecake recipe, you can find it in the appendix at the end of the book. But I warn you, it is complicated.

14

Lent 5 – Lazarus, Come Out!

"Lazarus... Lazarus... " she muttered, "Lazarus... *come out!*..."

Sid turns round, the tea towel in one hand still wrapped round the mug in his other. He looks at his wife, who sits frowning in furious concentration at the scrubbed top of the old pine table.

"I beg your pardon?" he says.

Rosie's head jerks up. He sees the flush of embarrassment redden her cheeks.

"Nothing," she says, hastily. "I didn't mean to say anything. I was just thinking."

Sid smiles. He finishes drying the mug, hangs it up on its hook under the pot shelf, shakes out the cloth and lays it over the back of a chair, and sits down opposite her, at the other end of the table.

"Thinking about what?" he says. You never know with Rosie.

He sees the fugitive expression flit across her face, looking for somewhere to hide. But he waits.

And eventually she says: "The thing is, Sid, I have to lose this weight. I weigh fifty-six – yes, *fifty-six* – pounds more than I did when I was a girl. I don't dance any more. I don't run. I even avoid bending down if I can. The floor is a long way down. I hate the sight of myself. I keep trying to tweak the details and the externals to improve things – different shoes, a new dress, some bright lipstick, a pair of showy earrings. It takes up all my spare money, and I look in the mirror and still I feel wretched. I think, 'Rosie, your face is horrible.' So I wonder if a haircut will do it, and I make an appointment, have it all snipped off into what they call a pixie cut. Ha! Some pixie! I come home, look in the mirror and a change is always welcome. For about two-and-a-half days I feel pleased. But there I am, every morning when I clean my teeth. More like a piggy than a pixie. Sid! Somewhere inside this tomb of flesh is a 140-pound woman with long hair. I've got to find her and get her out. I've got to unwrap these stuck clinging grave clothes of fat, fat, fat. I've got to get her out. If she can't slip insouciant through the world in her jeans, dancing to Janis Joplin and climbing up through the trees to the skyline, I'll lose her forever. Dead, Sid! She's dead! And I want her back."

Sid and Rosie have been married eight years. Not long in the scheme of things, but a lot of history happened before they found each other. Even so, in eight years he reckons he's probably packed in about twenty years' worth of listening. No, that's not fair. Make it fifteen.

He clears his throat cautiously.

"Now, my darling," he says – and observes Rosie's eyes take on that sharp look, always reminds him of a ferret, sort of sweet but lethal. He perseveres, soothingly. "My darling, you are beautiful to me. You're gorgeous. You don't need to lose anything. You look just as sexy, just as lovely, as ever you did. You look great with short hair. I adore your new dress and those pretty earrings… " But his voice tails off. Disdain and impatience are creeping into the eyes of the watching ferret. Clearly he has got this wrong. He tries again. "We all get older, Rosie. The pounds creep on with time. I've got a bit of a paunch these days, not to mention my hair seems to have somehow got down off the top of my head and is trying to creep out of my nose and ears undetected. It's OK. We can let youth go without – "

"No!" The ferret leaps, and Sid feels the harmless rabbit of his well-meant reasoning fall limp as sharp teeth sever its spinal cord.

"That's not it, Sid! I don't want to be young again, I don't want to be sexy, and I'm not doing this to please you! Somewhere inside me, entombed in fat, is a ten-stone woman, and I'm going to set her free. She's been there a while, she's been getting older waiting for me to come and look for her. But I'm going to get these grave clothes off her. I'm going to let her out. Before I die, before the light dims and the music fades, I'm going to bring her out here where she can dance just a little bit longer."

Sid nods, cautious. Better just listen, eh? He waits. Rosie's gaze drills into him still. He feels there is more to come.

"I took my mother out shopping on Thursday," she continues with apparent irrelevance. "You know how breathless she is now. Every few yards along the high street we have to stop and pretend to be captivated by some pointless shopfront while she struggles to get her breath. We were nearly back to the car park when we stopped outside the bakers. They had wedding cakes in the window and sausage rolls and macaroons and Victoria sponges. And Sid, they had Belgian buns. Gorgeous, sticky Belgian buns with currents and icing on top and a cherry. Enormous. Oh, Sid, I cannot tell you how much I wanted one of those Belgian buns. We stood there while her thin little chest heaved and she fought her way to equilibrium, ready to move on, and all the while my entire being was pouring through into one focus of longing and desire on that display of Belgian buns. All the way back to the car – she can only walk slowly, now – I went on seeing them. As I unlocked the doors and put my bag on the back seat, I was thinking, 'I could just run back and get one…' But I didn't. I got in the car and took her home. I drove back here for my salad."

Her eyes watch Sid. He looks back at her, acutely aware that he stands on the pinnacle of possibility for saying entirely the wrong thing. So he just nods.

"She is trapped inside me."

Who? wondered Sid, bewildered. *Your mother?*

"I have to force this body of flesh to offer up its fat to the gods of

74

determination and willpower. It's like the fat-offering in the book of Leviticus that has to be put on the altar and burned. I have to burn that fat. And it means I'll feel hungry and I'll drool as I imagine Belgian buns, but that's just how it is. I have to *eat myself*. I have to digest, metabolize, burn up, eat these grave clothes of fat and get this poor woman out where she can dance again. *I have to do it*, Sid!"

Blimey. Sid shifts in his chair. "OK… " he ventures warily. "Not… you'd rather… I perhaps not get you an Easter egg this year, then?"

She shakes her head, slowly. How can Rosie look so dangerous, he wonders.

"Sid," she persists. Uh-oh. He knows that persevering tone. He still hasn't got the point, has he? "Sid – isn't there something in you that the years have buried? Something that you can hardly remember but yearns to be set free? Isn't there an aspect of yourself that you let fall into neglect somewhere along the way, busy with earning money and raising children and doing all the practical, temporal stuff? A canary in a cage down in the mine of who you have become that deserves to be brought back to the surface again and set free?"

"Well…" Sid considers this. "I used to love going fishing. Sitting by the riverbank – the water, the trees, the birds singing, the sky. And playing golf. That was really exhilarating – I loved golf. But there doesn't really seem to be the time… I don't know. I just stopped."

"Exactly!" The ferret shakes its rabbit. "That's what I mean! Lazarus! *Come out!*"[26]

For sharing and wondering

- What makes you happy?
- Is there any one thing you would like to change about yourself?
- With the passing years, what aspects of your life or yourself can you identify as now very different from the person you once used to be?

---

26 John 11:43.

Into the Mystery

O great I AM, you have made us in your image, and given us lives and personalities to channel individually the myriad wonders of your glory. Help us to rejoice in how and who you have made us.

> *O God, grant us the serenity to accept the things we cannot change,*
> *The courage to change the things we can,*
> *And the wisdom to know the difference.*

Reinhold Niebuhr (1892–1971)

15

Feast of St Joseph

The meeting starts when the first person comes in and sits down. It's not yet half past ten, but four or five folk already sit motionless in the big, airy room. The bright, pale light of spring floods through the high Victorian windows. Outside, the gulls' wild cry and the gusting March wind. In here, quiet, peace profound.

Sid makes his way with no noise, between the shabby green chairs, across to the far corner on the bench where he likes to sit if it's free. Always this gladness when he comes to meeting, as if a band were removed from around his heart. In meeting, he stops trying and just is. Here, he doesn't do anything more than open… open… open… like a sea anemone, like a mesembryanthemum in full sun, like a baby bird's beak awaiting worms. He opens his whole self and lets the Light pour in, drinking thirstily, gratefully, as if he could never get enough. This is where Sid renews his hope. Thou leadest me by still waters… in green pastures… thou restorest my soul… my cup runneth over… surely goodness and mercy will follow me all the days of my life.[27] He settles himself comfortably into this, his corner, and closes his eyes. When I am old, Sid thinks, I'd like to die right here. How wonderful that would be.

From time to time he hears the door on its spring shush open and shut, as Friends enter and take their places. Sid has no words for the way this gathering moves him; something casual and heartening, like

27   Psalm 23.

family, a kind of belonging. No ritual, no procession, no hierarchy; only gathering, and waiting, and Light. Most Sundays there is not even spoken ministry, just silence. But the silence is not empty – Sid smiles at the very thought. Down, down, down the Friends travel together into the silence, as momentous as a fairground ride, this plunge into the darksome Light. Deeper and deeper into the silence they go, feel the gathering, feel the meeting. Gee, thinks Sid sometimes, this is... why – this is like sex! So intimate, so deep, so loving is the silence and the union; so profound. At the end, up they rise together, up, up, like divers coming up together, twisting and turning in the weightless silence, swimming up towards the Light fracturing and sparkling above. Then they break surface with a leap of exultation, all the more intense for the quietness in which it is held. With an inward smile of utter satisfaction, one Friend turns to another to shake hands. How powerful silence is. It asks more of a soul than most are willing to give; few will try to plumb Quaker silence. But those who taste it, love it, rely on it, find satisfaction and even intoxication. No. That's not the right word for this beautiful pure encounter, thinks Sid. Not intoxication – there is nothing toxic about this. Elation, then. Euphoria.

He withdraws his mind from wandering along these tracks of thought, and allows himself just to feel the meeting, the arising angel of the gathering. He opens his eyes and glances round. Ten forty. The room almost full. Then, to his surprise, his gaze falls upon strangers, seated in the far corner of the room. He knows most everybody who comes to meeting – by sight at least – but this little family he has never seen before. A man, a woman, and a child.

The woman is slight, somewhat fragile. The pallor of her face contrasts starkly with the waves of dark hair framing it, falling to her thin shoulders in their warm woollen sweater. Round her closed eyes, Sid recognizes the blue shadows of tiredness. Just looking at her brings back memories of life with an infant in the household. He cannot see her hands from where he sits, but thinks they must be clasped loosely in her lap. She looks not sleepy, but as though the silence is resting her – what she needs. Beside her, clearly *with* her – the whole side of his arm in companionable contact with the side of hers, a man whose face Sid loves at first sight. His eyes too are closed, his mien composed into peace unfathomable. The stranger has long brown hair – longer than hers – and a glossy brown beard of competition length, tucked to one side of the little one sound asleep in the enfolding baby wrap the man wears; one of those modern – or possibly ancient, traditional – slings. Baby-wearing. Sid knows about this. His daughter does it, and he carried her the same way when she, too, was a child, because he was a bit of a hippy back then, more involved than most fathers in the care of their children.

It's Mary and Joseph, Sid thinks, and this brings a smile to his face. He likes the idea that when Jesus is present in the meeting, it is with the serene innocence of a sleeping child. All right, not that only – Christ challenges with full authority and cuts pretension to the heart as he meets Friends here in the silence – but what a vision of peace even so.

Sid grew up Roman Catholic – not until his adult life did he encounter the Friends. He knows and loves St Joseph, husband of Mary, of old. He knows that Joseph passes through the entire Gospel story in Quakerly silence, never uttering a single word. That Christ, the living Word of God is the adopted son of kind and hospitable silence. Joseph's silence is not the hostile or sulky variety, it is a listening silence, capable of dreaming the desires of God, submitting his spirit to what life asks of him, regardless of ridicule or disappointment. He didn't have to marry Mary, the girl with Christ in her belly. The silence of Joseph receives the infant Word, forms and nourishes and matures the Word until it reaches readiness to issue forth in ministry. St Joseph, Sid thinks, was probably the first Quaker.

The child held close in the wrap stirs a little, emitting the gentle musical sigh of sleep. Sid's Joseph has his hands placed lightly round the little body, protective, reassuring. Silence protects and nurtures a newborn Word.

In these moments – how has that happened? An hour has gone by! – Sid feels the meeting beginning to rise, rise up through the silence in communion. Across the room, the bearded man wearing the baby opens his eyes. Straight into each other's eyes they look, Sid and this stranger. Naturally, unforced by social expectation, the silence between them forms into a smile.

Then everyone is shaking hands.

When the afterthoughts and notices are done, Sid gets to his feet. He won't stay for coffee today. Friends are gathered round the strangers, getting them drinks, making them welcome; but Sid heads out for the street. He doesn't wait to discover what their real names are. For this morning at least he wants to savour the wonder that Mary and Joseph came to meeting, and brought their baby with them. Today the best of all happened; the heart of the silence bore the living Word.

For sharing and wondering

- What has been your experience/observation of bringing children and babies to church?
- Sid thinks he'd like to die in Quaker meeting, one day when he's old. If you could pick the circumstance of your death, what would you choose?
- What have been your experiences of profound silence?

Into the Mystery

The whole of our lives, your love holds us and your wisdom guides us, in utter silence. Help us to become so comfortable and familiar with silence that we hear your voice more clearly every day.

16

Holy Week

It is Holy Week.

"This is the only time," says Rosie, "when I feel uncomfortable about not going to church."

Sid asks the obvious. "Why don't you go, then?"

"You know why. It goes on too long and I'm OK until about a third of the way through and then this feeling seizes me that I have to get out, get out, and I can't stand it. It's the people vibe, the heaving sea of all of what they are, their restlessness. And the choice is mostly between the minister's badly put together personal angle or ritualism that stifles the moving of the Spirit. No depth, Sid."

"So... why feel uncomfortable about staying away?"

"Because I can't bear the idea of leaving Jesus to die alone."

"But, you just said, about the heaving sea of people. He's not alone."

"The heaving sea is what's inside them, nothing to do with numbers. Unresolved issues, curiosity, random thoughts, untamed emotion. Besides, on one level – much as the phrase is reviled nowadays – there really is just Jesus and me. Either I'm with him, or I'm not. It doesn't matter what anyone else is doing."

"Fair enough. Well – how about this for an idea? The Society of Friends doesn't do Holy Week, and that makes me feel uneasy too. I mean how can you not keep vigil at the cross? This is where my Catholic roots run above the ground, I guess. So how about you and

I light a candle here on the kitchen table every day this week, and every morning we can take a few minutes to have our own Quaker silence, and then share our thoughts about what it all might mean? Would that sit right?"

Rosie thinks about it, and nods slowly. "I'd like that," she says. "Can we start now? I'll go and get a tea light if you just bundle the cereal bowls into the sink."

She brings a candle in a saucer, and goes into the garden to gather a few leaves and early flowers, and they sit in quietness together, resting in the peace of the simple flame, the silence, the artless imperfection of blossom and twig. The presence of Jesus is with them, the familiar warmth of his courage and kindness, shining through even the sombre gravity of this season, its shadows, its cruelty, its fear and horror. A time when the groaning of all the world's anguish twists up to a crescendo.

After a while has gone by, into the silence Rosie says, "Wu-wei."

Sid wonders if that's it or there's more to come. He asks himself if this is like Quaker meeting and you just accept the ministry for what it is, or if she intended to begin a conversation. "Woo-who?" he wonders, but thinks that might sound flippant and hurt the solemnity of the moment they had found.

"Explain?" he asks softly.

"Chinese. It's a concept from the Tao. They call it 'the art of non-doing'. In the *Tao Te Ching*, Lao Tsu says that when you follow the Way – because Tao means Way; it's the ordinary Chinese word for a street – you don't acquire skill, cleverness, acumen, whatever. You don't acquire at all. Bit by bit you drop everything, until you have nothing. And when you have nothing, you have everything. When nothing is done, nothing is left undone.[28] Wu-wei is the centre point, like the eye of the storm, a place where no action is taken but everything is achieved. The perfect heart of the will of God. Just being there."

28 See *Tao Te Ching*, chapter 48.

Sid listens carefully. "Is that... I think that's the same as 'passion'?" he suggests tentatively. "As in, the Passion of Jesus. It comes from the Latin. Same root as 'passive' – allowing something, letting it happen. And it's what 'suffer' means, too. Like he said, 'Suffer the little children to come unto me.'[29] It means 'to allow'. The Passion of Jesus is his surrendering himself, permitting the agony of what had to be – God's perfect love – to course through him. So he was silent before Pilate when he asked him, 'What is truth?' Jesus just stood there quietly, and the answer was greater than a formulation of words, it was the silence of his presence, all of him, the chance to look into his eyes. The 'I Am' that is the only possible answer to 'What is truth?' Is... is it like that, you mean – that Chinese thing?"

"Wu-wei. Exactly that. And then, in the *Tao*, Lao Tsu also speaks of the Valley Spirit.[30] He identifies it as like the mother of all that is, the feminine principle. But men can have the Valley Spirit, it's not just for women. It's the cradle of life, a place of fertility – a valley. Where the living water flows to the sea. Where the trees and all the tender plants can grow. The tree of life for the healing of the nations.[31] The Valley Spirit never dies, Lao Tsu says. And I think that was the unquenchable thing about Jesus. The light that shone in the darkness, and the darkness couldn't engulf it or understand it. The darkness was too dim to snuff it out. He died, of course. He was beaten and tortured and put to death. But the Valley Spirit, which is humility, life-giving, can never die. That is inherently impossible, because it is life – it is the mother of everything. Resurrection belongs to it."

Sid sits quietly, listening, thinking about what she is saying, looking at the candle flame and the inconsequential flowers and leaves with their casual beauty, at the bare wood of the table, scrubbed and scarred and weathered by decades of use. They got it second hand, it was old already, a place where ordinary families had gathered since Victorian days.

29 For example, Matthew 19:14.
30 See *Tao Te Ching*, chapter 6.
31 See Revelation 22 and see also Ezekiel 47.

"Lao Tsu says the sea is the king of a hundred streams because it lies below them,"[32] Rosie says. "It's the wu-wei of creation. All it has to do is just be, and everything comes to it. Everything flows in to the lowest place. 'How blessed are the meek: for they shall inherit the earth.'[33] Learning to trust enough to accept and receive what life offers, what must be, even when that is painful and difficult – even when it's pure agony."

Sid frowns slightly and shifts in his chair. "Not to be masochistic, though," he counters. "Not to encourage people to disrespect you. There's a difference between being the sea with all the rivers flowing into it and being the council dump with garbage trucks arriving every minute."

"Well, I'm not sure," says Rosie, "but I *think* wu-wei takes care of that. I think when you arrive at the place Jesus was at, of absolute humility and simplicity, of transparent truth, a condition of integrity in its fullest meaning – the shalom of God – then whatever life throws at you just integrates as well. Like when he touched the people with leprosy, and instead of him getting leprosy they got what he had. That's the I Am – all he had to do was be."

She falls silent, then draws breath to speak again, but glances at Sid, worried she may be doing too much talking. "Go on," he says.

"I was just thinking of that thing Julian of Norwich said – 'I chose Jesus for my heaven, and him in all his passion and grief'."[34]

Sid closes his eyes. "Jesus," he says softly, "Jesus… please be in me."

For sharing and wondering

- How do you recharge your batteries? Would that mostly be in solitude or in the company of other people?

- How do you foster a servant spirit without becoming a doormat?

32 See Tao Te Ching, chapter 66.
33 Matthew 5:5.
34 Julian of Norwich, Revelations of Divine Love.

- Can you describe a time when you felt the presence of Jesus for yourself?

Into the Mystery

At the foot of the cross, we draw close to you, Jesus, Redeemer of the world. We adore you in the passion of your love, in the agony of your dying, in your abandonment to the Father's good purposes, in the emptying of all self-interest from your soul.

17

Easter

"Sid," says Rosie, "why is Easter called Easter? 'Christmas' makes sense, and 'Candlemas' too – once you know about the old pagan traditions of lighting a candle in every room of the house at Imbolc – but what's with 'Easter'? It isn't anything-mas. What does it mean?"

"Oh, it's quite beautiful!" Sid looks up from his crossword, eagerness in his face. "Beautiful and very interesting. It's like following a winding, twisty little path through the trees, and suddenly coming to a sunny, open glade in the middle of the forest.

"Easter is all proto-Germanic and Old English and Dark Ages stuff. Glorious. OK, if you go right back to Proto-Indo-European, there's a word-root, *aus-*, and it means 'to shine'. It's where our word 'east' derives from. And of course the sun rises in the east, hence the Proto-Germanic development austrōn, meaning 'dawn'. From there it passed into Old English as *Ēostre*, the name of a goddess of the dawn. The Venerable Bede, writing in the eighth century says there was a special month – *Eosturmonath* – devoted to the goddess Ēostre in the Anglo-Saxon calendar. It corresponds with what we now call 'April' – a Roman name of obscure origin, possibly something to do with the Greek goddess Aphrodite.

"Jacob Grimm turned up an Old High German form, Ostara, and identifies an Old High German adverb, *ôstar*, which describes movement towards the rising sun. It has a Norse equivalent, *austr*, and there's an Old Norse form of the goddess to go with it – Austra.

So this is a deity of the rising sun's radiance. Perhaps something not a million miles from what the ancient Hebrews called the *shekinah* – the radiance of God in creation. Ostara is the old Celtic quarter day – the spring equinox, the balancing of the light with the darkness. Lady Day is settled just nearby, of course, on 25 March – making quiet connections between Mary who brought forth Jesus from her womb, with the goddess of new life who turns her face to the rising sun, welcoming the birth of the light from the mystery of the darkness.

"The resurrection of Jesus was actually at that time of the year, so it makes sense to celebrate it then, but if you put it all together with Christ being called the Morning Star, and the Day Star – terms for the sun, obviously – then you can see how it would fit just right."

"This goddess," says Rosie, "presumably has links with the word 'oestrogen'?"

"Well, I think there must be a connection. The etymologists don't say so. *Oestrus* – which oestrogen comes from, is a word for female animals coming into heat – being ready to mate. Which is all about fertility and new life – hence, presumably, the custom associating eggs with Easter. The ancient, pre-Christian religions saw springs – water sources – as holy. The word for a spring was *os*, which is the name given to the neck of the cervix in a woman's womb. The Earth was a mother, source of life, and a spring represented the opening of her womb. That's why places where springs were are given names like Ladywell and Osmotherly – they were appropriated for Our Lady the Mother of Jesus, from their pagan origins. And sunrise is referred to as 'dayspring' sometimes – it is the same mystery; life out of the dark earth, light born anew from the night sky. The symbolism of Christ emerging from the tomb as an archetype of life brought forth from the womb of Earth, the rising sun and everything – it's all of a bundle, isn't it?"

"Gosh, yes. But Jesus rising from the dead is in a different category, surely. I mean, whatever an agnostic or devotee of another religion may think, Christians believe the resurrection is an actual historical event – whereas an archetype would be like, legend – wouldn't it?"

Sid frowns, thinking. "Not... not exactly. An archetype recurs as a pattern or a theme because it's a central, essential, underlying reality. It's kind of causative. An archetype is about *truth*. Archetypes stand behind, rather than proceeding from, the legends of different social cultures.

"And the thing about truth is that it is multi-dimensional – however you approach it, a truth remains consistent. So the truth of Christ's presence in God's creation is cosmic – it pre-dates all human existence, never mind human society. Christ's participation in the radiance of God, his creative Word, the emanation of life as light – this is how the universe was *made*. And still we encounter God as light. Even Buddhists and Quakers, who are ambivalent about theism to put it mildly, can warm to the idea of the numinous experience of light.

"The Christ who comes forth as light and life from the deadness of the grave; the sun rising in splendour from behind the eastern rim of the Earth, dispelling the darkness; the concept of a dawn goddess ripe and full of the promise of life – they are *inevitable*, if you see what I mean. How Jesus fits into history will not sit at odds with the insights and intimations of the divine gleaned throughout all the millennia. It's a fulfilment, not a contradiction. And I tell you what, the church simply doesn't need this adversarial, paranoid stance it's adopted in recent times, determined to prove everybody else wrong about every mortal thing. In my opinion, it's time the church got the habit of celebrating truth wherever it can be found. That's what the old Celtic church used to do, which is why we have 'Easter' and not 'Risingmas' or 'Lifefest'. There was a time when the company of the friends of Jesus had enough faith in his strength and life and power not to be touchy and defensive about proximity with other folks' religions. They thought all truth was God's truth – and they were right; so it is."

"All right, Sid – calm down! I get it!"

He smiles. "I know, I'm sorry. I do get het up about this. It's because I think if there's one thing human beings need above all else it's the ability to work together. Religion is the cause of so many wars – the stupid waste of life and hope, of resources and happiness, of every blessed thing that makes life worth living. If only we could agree to stop arguing and fighting about our creeds and doctrines, and be simply glad to lift our faces to the light that enlightens every man[35] – and *every woman*, of course, Rosie! Gee! I don't want to start *another* war!"

For sharing and wondering

- What attracted you to the Christian faith – and what has ever put you off it?
- Think of five principles of good practice for missionaries.
- At Quaker meeting, some are Christians, some theists, some are neither. How would you feel about belonging to a meeting for worship where there was not necessarily any agreement on religious belief?

Into the Mystery

Risen Lord Jesus, with what gladness we greet you! May your new life rise up irresistibly in our own hearts and minds, until the ordinary circumstances of our everyday lives shine with the radiance of your presence.

---

35   John 1:9.

18

Living the Ascension

"The Ascension – " Sid swirls his wine thoughtfully in his glass, gazing moodily into its dark ruby depths – "Jeepers! I mean, what are we meant to do with it? Where do we go with that?"

"What?" Rosie, sitting beside him on the garden bench, her feet up on its matching table, eats another olive from the glazed terracotta bowl on the tray between them. "D'you mean, what use is the concept for practical purposes?"

She turns her head to see his reaction, squinting against the rays of the low evening sun. Sid nods. "Yes," he says. He hears the eagerness steal into her body, her voice, her mind, as she starts, "Oh! Well – "

Her enthusiasm brings a smile into his eyes.

"Ascension is *ever so* practical! It's just the best thing!" Sid knows he has the dish of olives all to himself for now.

"One of the most destructive things in life is, surely, clinging," she says. "If we cling to what's tried and true it feels safe, but we miss so much – it stops us growing and changing, developing. If we cling to the past in nostalgia we become discontented and ill-adjusted, unable to embrace the here and now. Goodness me, the number of churches I've had to do with that simply *could not* let go of the past! Not useful things of the past, I mean, like wisdom heritage – a fine preaching tradition or a body of theological scholarship – no, just types of seating or old buildings past their use-by date, or old

90

artefacts of indifferent quality. Nostalgia – oh, it's a killer! Like the cobwebs that tangle the unwary butterfly.

"Of course, it's just as easy to get mired in *bad* memories of the past – like Aunt Ada Doom and her 'I saw something nasty in the woodshed';[36] making things that befell us long ago our excuse for settling for less ever afterward.

"Life only becomes possible in any real sense if we're willing to move on. And that can cost everything. Think of a caterpillar. It has to dissolve – actually become *liquid* inside the chrysalis if it ever wants to become a butterfly. You have to let go of the past, of what you know, of the comfortable familiar. It's the only way.

"If you want to make any progress in any kind of spiritual discipline whatsoever, you also have to let go of physical stuff – what you own and even your body. All of us get sick, all of us will die one day – and so will everyone we love. Clinging is pointless, because impermanence is part of the human condition. We have to learn to let go.

"And *things* – our possessions – people think they're inert, lifeless, but it isn't so. I kid you not, every mortal thing you own, it has an agenda, needs, it calls to you, claims you. The only way truly to be free is to *get rid of it* – cut free, travel light, walk through life like a pilgrim. Clutter, memorabilia – all our hoards; they are not neutral, they interfere with our freedom, weigh us down. I promise you, this is true.

"Some of our clutter can't be itemized materially – it's status, achievement, snobbery; or a cluttered schedule, a crammed diary. These are all forms of clinging, Sid. Neediness gone mad.

"And then there's clinging relationships – whether that's in terms of manipulation or toxic codependency or bearing grudges or just being unwilling to move on. Situations where people drained of love trudge resentfully along together, unwilling to do the soul work to get to understanding and tenderness, or forgive and cut loose.

36   From Stella Gibbons's 1932 comedic novel, Cold Comfort Farm.

"God is Spirit, and in his presence is fullness of joy. Where his reign begins, it brings liberty – lightness. Clinging is probably the closest thing to Hell imaginable.

"So, there you have Jesus, fresh out of the tomb, recently crucified. Betrayed and abandoned by his friends and fellow Israelites, let down by his government, tortured. What's not to resent? Blame, recrimination, offended hurt, would seem to be the order of the day. And it was no light thing, that suffering. It passed into his very *identity*. Even in his risen body, the scars of the nails and spear became his badge, what made him recognizable. But he left that behind, somehow; he knew how to let it go. He didn't come back snarling, all ready for red-hot revenge; he was able to move on.

"Not everyone felt the same. Mary, wanting to cling to the man she loved, in the garden; Thomas wanting to put his fingers into the nail-prints, the spear-scar. They had no vision for anything bigger – they just longed for the same old same old; our Jesus, back again just like before.

"But he said, don't cling to me – I am not yet ascended to the Father. I doubt they could make much sense of that, and nor can most people who don't appreciate how lethal a drug is clinging, that deadens the spirit and binds us into the material realm.

"When he left, when he ascended, you'd have thought that was simply the end. Finito, Benito. Gone. Turned out, it was just the beginning. It showed what he meant about the seed falling into the ground and dying to allow the harvest to come. That wasn't about his physical death and resurrection only, it included letting go of everything – relationships, the concentration of the Spirit in his own person, the whole lot. As it turned out, the incarnation of God in Jesus was a stage in an unfolding process, the creation of an open way linking Earth to heaven for all time.

"The Ascension must have seemed like a loss, a disaster – a second whammy after they lost him at the crucifixion. How could they have predicted it would open the floodgates for Pentecost, the outpouring of the Holy Spirit on humankind once the way had been opened?

"And what is true of Jesus is always true of us too, because he was as human as we are. If we can find courage and love and hope – just like he did – to let the old stuff go; everything, the relationships, the achievements, the loves and the wounds, the betrayals and the friendships, all the ground we gained, even life itself – then the way opens to blessings unimagined. We make space for the Spirit to pour through.

"I mean, how can anyone say that isn't practical? Living the Ascension is the most useful, realistic, life-affirming path it is possible for anyone to take. Plus it cultivates trust, in life and in God; it says 'I believe', unwaveringly, through whatever circumstances conspire to throw at you."

Sid looks at the last olive in the dish, hesitates, then pops it in his mouth. He sets his emptied wine glass down on the tray. "I thought you'd know, if I asked," he says, glad he married this rather odd but very articulate woman.

He gets to his feet slowly, conscious of being more creaky than once he was.

"I'll put the pasta on," he says, looking down at her, loving her. "The sauce is all ready. We can eat out here."

He moves to go, then pauses, thinking. "This business of living the Ascension," he says, "it's not all for the ultimate and the life hereafter, is it? If you can let go of all the clutter and clinging, let go of the past – well, it makes space for life and loving here and now, too, doesn't it? It makes room for today."

"Well, I've always thought so," she says. "Bring some more olives out with the pasta, would you, my darling?"

For sharing and wondering

- Do you enjoy eating outdoors? Or does the sun get in your eyes, the sand in your sandwiches and every mosquito in the neighbourhood try to join in?

- Make a list of your possessions that you regard as essential, and a list of reasons why you keep the things that are not.

- What things – happy or sad, physical or invisible – might it be time for you to let go of now, after carrying them with you a long time?

Into the Mystery

Help us to travel light on this pilgrimage with you, walking Jesus, ascending Jesus. You were born under a star, you slept many a night under the stars, and you ascended to the stars in the end. May the freedom and mystery of the cosmic scale on which you live illuminate the ordinary fabric of our day-to-day detail of our lives.

19

Beltane

"I sometimes wonder," says Sid, "to what extent someone's religion determines their life, and to what extent it's the other way round."

"Like what the Sea of Faith people believe?"[37] Rosie looks up from the blanket she is crocheting, which has grown to enormous technicolour proportions. "Like Don Cupitt and friends? They think God has no objective, intrinsic existence, don't they? That what we call 'God' is the sum of our values, unified into a metaphor and projected as an actual being. What they call 'demythologized'. What I call 'made up'."

Sid laughs. "Goodness me, I'm not sure I would want to line up behind Don Cupitt! If I've understood him correctly, he's in favour of religion without God, where I think I'd prefer God without religion. I believe he went on to conjecture that not only is God not real but nothing else is real either. Including Don Cupitt, presumably. The living definition of a man who vanished up his own backside. But no – that wasn't what I meant. I was thinking about Beltane."

"Beltane?" Rosie has heard this word. It's an old Celtic festival, she knows, but she could hazard no further guess than that.

"Yes, it's one of the cross-quarter days. You know: the quarter days are the two solstices and the equinoxes, and then the cross-quarter days come halfway between those festivals. Beltane is after Ostara at the equinox and before Litha at midsummer.

37 An organization exploring and promoting religious faith as a human creation.

95

"What specially interests me about it is that it came to be so significant. The cross-quarter days were fire festivals, and of the four of them, Beltane and Samhain became the most important. They pretty much divided the year. Beltane was in effect the threshold of the summer, and Samhain at the end of October was the threshold of the winter. It reminds me of the monastic offices of lauds and vespers. They were known as the 'cardinal offices', and acquired particular importance. 'Cardinal' comes from the Latin, *cardo*, which means 'hinge'. Lauds and vespers got that name because they opened and closed the day. They weren't the first and last offices in the twenty-four-hour cycle, but they were the sunrise and sunset offices, so lay people – villagers – often attended them. Like sheep to the fold. Out of these offices the Church of England's matins and evensong grew, and were observed in every parish, every day.

"In *The Golden Bough*,[38] Sir James Frazer makes the point that although Beltane and Samhain don't come at a significant time for arable farms across Europe, they were immensely important occasions for herdsmen. So he thinks their comparative consequence is an indication that they grew up at a time when the Celtic world was primarily pastoral, dependent on its flocks and herds."

"Interesting," says Rosie. "I bet he's right. Sounds likely, doesn't it? What did they do at Beltane, then?"

Sid smiles. "It seems no festival was quite complete, in the ancient Celtic opinion, without a dirty great big bonfire. And at no time was this more so than at Beltane. It was the time when the cattle were driven out to their summer pastures. They used to drive them between two sacred fires, or in some cases make them jump over the fires or the embers, or just had them pass the fire and blow the smoke over them."

"Fumigation?" Rosie wonders. "The stables where they over-wintered might have been a good place for fleas to hide."

---

38 The Golden Bough by the Scottish anthropologist Sir James George Frazer, first published in 1890, is a comprehensive study of mythology and religion, examining religion as a cultural phenomenon rather than taking a theological stance.

"You see, now you're thinking like I am," says Sid. "That the fires might have been sacred, but they had a pragmatic component as well. There were prayers and rituals to do with the protection of the livestock, and in the Scottish highlands they cooked a kind of eggnog over the bonfires, and offered it as a libation to the fox, the eagle – all the predators that might harm the farm animals. The day began at sundown, remember, so on Beltane Eve everyone's candles and hearth fires would be doused, and then lit again the next day, at the end of the festival, from the sacred fire.

"It has so many resonances with Christian tradition, doesn't it? The paschal fire that we light in the Catholic church at the Easter vigil. From the fire, the priest lights the paschal candle with the five pins for the five wounds of Christ pressed into it. Then he holds it up, and there's the spine-chillingly triumphant triple chant announcing the delivery of light from darkness, the birth of new life. It has a versicle: 'Lumen Christi!'[39] The response of the people is, 'Deo Gratias!'[40] Then there's the fire of the Holy Spirit at Pentecost, not to mention the burnt offerings of the Old Testament and the blood of the lamb on the lintel for the protection of the people of God.

"When you think about it, you can see how these potent symbols – fire, light, food – touch upon the basic necessities of human well-being. *Of course* they become the heart of our religious practice."

Rosie ponders these words, starting a new row in a deep, rich shade of red. "I suppose it's reasonable that Don Cupitt and friends should have concluded there's nothing more to religion than the sum total of human experience," she says. "Creatures of Earth projecting their fears and vulnerability, hopefully, up to the silent stars."

"Depends how your mind works," says Sid. "We earthlings are bound to be preoccupied with survival. And our imagination is bound to be taken up with what we know – sun, wind, fire, water, trees, birds, animals. But as to Don Cupitt and the Sea of Faith – I think they've got the whole thing back to front. Religion, in the

39 "The Light of Christ!"
40 "Thanks be to God!"

end, is merely our response. Faith begins with an experience of the numinous. The natural world – sunlight dappling through the summer leaves, snowflakes, sparks flying upward into the darkness – are the interface, the means by which God speaks into a physical world. Creation is a sort of language: 'In the beginning was the Word'.[41] All we do, the paschal candle, the holy fire, the cup of wine raised up, the bread broken – it's not a projection. Its direction is not travelling upward from us, taking shape as some emergent deity. It's the other way round. This is the bowl we fashion, the cupped hand we lift, the beak we open, to receive our viaticum – our food for the journey – Holy Spirit, the anointing of the living God."

For sharing and wondering

- What childhood memories do you have of firelight?
- If there were no church to go to, what ceremonies would you put in place to observe your faith. Would they have songs, spoken prayers, silence, candles, flowers, or… ? Would they be at meal times, the ending and beginning of the day, every day or just sometimes, or… ?
- To what extent do you think the faith of the church has been revealed to us by God, and to what extent have we sanctified norms that grew out of our own culture?

Into the Mystery

Living God, your creative word sang the cosmos into being, and your Spirit breathes and speaks and shines through every raindrop, every falling leaf, every silent stone. Help us to live with the eyes of our spirits open, to discern your presence and make you welcome in the temple of our hearts.

41 John 1:1.

20

Pentecost

There they are. Sid's angels. Cruising lazily round the garden as he stands looking up, his hand raised to shield his eyes against the sun. Then here they come floating down, blessings of shadow and night, of inscrutable mystery, their wings outspread, the furthest pinions separate and up-curving like fingertips. Such magnificent crows.

Alighted on the grass they come forward eagerly, trusting him, to the dish he has set down for them: shredded meat and fish rejected by picky cats. They take it in turns to watch and eat, eat and watch.

Sid thinks of this as his thank you for the ravens who fed humanity, bringing bread and meat for Elijah in his hungry wilderness. Here you are, little human – eat that. So now Sid brings bread and meat for the crows; the relationship abides.

It began in the wintertime, when Sid and Rosie made sure to put out food for all the creatures visiting their garden. The badger, short-sighted and regular in his habits, snuffling across the grass, eager for meat and anything with a taste of honey. The small birds clustering on the grain feeder, squabbling and fluttering, pecking like mad at the swaying coconut shell dangling on a length of rough twine, full of seed-packed hard white fat. The bigger song-birds hopping bright-eyed along the garden wall, heads cocked to the side, glad of bread and crumbled cheese. The vixen, appearing from nowhere, dancing on silent feet, glance missing nothing, hungry for scraps of anything, anything. On the roof of the woodstore Rosie scatters stale bread; swooping seagulls gobble it as if they were starving, gulping it in lumps down their bulging throats. The instant they take off, the magpies or the pigeons close in for what's left over. Down on the stone flags, darting swift and brief from the shelter of the logs, small rodents with jewel eyes and trembling whiskers glean the final crumbs.

But after a while Sid knew to look out for this particular pair of crows, and – which intrigued him – soon he realized everybody else knew to look out for them too. Every morning now he comes out after breakfast with the blue bowl of left-over cat food, and scans the sky for them. There they'll be, perched in the topmost branches of a tall ash two gardens away, watching for him. He retreats, but even so the seagulls and magpies, who used to snatch the cat food in an instant, cease to come. They watch still from rooftops and high branches, but word has got round it seems; this treat belongs to the crows alone – it is theirs, and that has to be respected.

The pair of crows, the feathers of their broad shoulders gleaming in the sunlight, share the feast. When they're done, they take flight again, but they don't leave straight away. They pause on the wall, on a limb of the old apple tree, and cry a word of thanks to Sid before their final departure.

Sid likes it that his crows always stop to say thank you, and he appreciates their mode of appearing too. Sid is interested in cultural differences around the world, and he read one time about how brash and presumptuous it seems to an Indian, the way an Englishman will stride right up to a neighbour's house, banging on the door for attention. The Indian thinks a more polite approach is to hover in the street just outside the gate, waiting to be noticed and invited in. Sid likes the courtesy of his crows, waiting in the tree nearby (but not too near), chatting loudly in hope of attracting his attention, yet never so pushy as to camp out right there in his garden demanding breakfast. The corvine etiquette pleases him.

And he marvels at the web of communication he has stumbled

upon – that the other birds in the neighbourhood (even the gluttonous, mannerless gulls) have evidently either been informed or surmised for themselves that Sid means this food for his crows, and so it shall be. He loved it in the early days of this relationship, when one of the pair would keep watch on the ridge tiles of his house while the other flew down to eat. If he came into the garden, the lookout would call a warning to the feasting bird. If he took a step further, the watcher would call again; and again if he took a step back – and each call slightly different. Sid had to acknowledge, this was language. And now when they pause on the wall before leaving his garden each morning, crying their raucous farewell, again his soul is moved to wonder; language – this is language, this is speech.

On Pentecost Sunday, Sid accepts Rosie's invitation to go along to the Anglican church for a change. He makes himself comfortable in the corner of the pew and hears again the story of how the Spirit came. He closes his eyes, and tries to imagine the wind and the fire. The picture conjured in his mind is of a pinioned bird, a crow in fact, not black but all gleaming like bright flame, fiery feathers ruffling in the breeze, riding the wind currents to float down from a far treetop, unhurried and assured, coming to land at last on the household of God.

As the preacher goes on with his message, about how Babel rudely scattered human communication but in the Spirit the web is woven once again, Sid's thoughts drift. He wonders about the gift of tongues and how far its territory might stretch. To be understood by everyone in his own native tongue – what a gift! Sid probes with longing the possibility of making himself understood with crows… woodmice… gulls… foxes…

To understand, and to be understood. He turns over and over in his mind this possibility, and it seems to him a pearl of great price; a gift indeed. Rosie, he thinks, understands him. She can read his mood. "What's wrong Sid?" she will ask of one silence, but snuggle close to a different silence with the contentment of a purring cat. He need say nothing. She hears the voiceless language of his soul.

Sid's thoughts range across the expanses of the universe, spanning time and space until they come to the world's first morning, where everything starts with the breath of God, with a word, speech, an utterance – "Let there be light." The Earth and everything in it is made out of the language of God; all creation speaks God's language, the word of the Spirit from which liquid illumination flows, enlightenment.

He wonders if the separation of man from his world is what it means to be fallen – to be set apart from the web of life that came singing out of the speaking breath, Spirit, of God. He turns over the possibility of what it can mean that God was in Jesus reconciling all creation to himself, making it whole again, restoring the pattern, the communion. He is not sure. He feels himself to be in deep waters.

But in the morning garden Sid lifts up his eyes unto the hills, from whence, like Noah's raven returning to him after millennia, comes drifting down on graceful wing this inchoate embodiment of word inarticulate. As the Spirit comes, as life comes home to itself, so in this establishment of unexpected trust Sid feels the granulating of creation, Christ's reconciliation.

Watching this crow, Sid remembers he is not the first to look on creation and feel an upwelling of delight, in the impulse that says, "Ain't that *good!*"

For sharing and wondering

- What animals and birds can you see from the windows of your home?
- How do you think the fall of man shows itself in our world, and where can you see the signs of redemption and the coming of the kingdom?
- How do you think the church should model, for society, a sense of responsibility for the wellbeing of creation?

Into the Mystery

Help us, good Lord, to love you in what you have made. May your grace be at work in us to protect the woodlands and wetlands, the rivers and wild places, the oceans and hills. Lead us into simplicity so the Earth's resources are not exhausted. Open our eyes to wonder at how precious and how glorious is this little planet teeming with so many kinds of life.

21

Trinity Sunday – Emergent Deity

On this radiant day of pouring sunshine and lofty unsurpassable blue ringing with birdsong, Sid has been working in the garden, and now he feels hungry. He stands upright – slowly, one hand pressed to his back – takes off the necessary gloves with which he has been pulling nettles, and heads towards the kitchen.

Indoors he stands and listens. Sublime music, building and towering like gathering clouds, is happening in the living room. Sid potters along the passage, and puts his head round the door. Rosie is lying flat on her back in the middle of the carpet, her eyes closed, rapt in the glories of William Byrd's three-part Mass – evidently asking about lunch would be unwise. She is up to the *Credo*. "*Deum de Deo* …" sing the three interweaving voices: "… *Lumen de Lumine…* "

Sid withdraws, silently pulling shut the door, to leave her in peace with the music. Back in the kitchen, he opens the fridge, finds an apple and some cheese. He gets the dish of butter and the jar of plum chutney from the larder, and the remaining half-loaf of olive ciabatta. He pours himself a glass of chilled beer for this hot day. This meal is looking good.

Deum de Deo… he thinks to himself as he takes down a plate from the shelf: *Lumen de Lumine…*

He takes quiet pleasure in finding a link between his Catholic

104

roots and the Quaker flowering of his faith. Light of Light. Light proceeding from Light. Light begotten by Light. He thinks of Brian McClaren's ideas about "emergent church" – something altogether more provisional and fluid than the traditional understandings of the faith community, nothing like as evermore-shall-be-so. Surveying the food assembling satisfactorily on his plate, he twists round on the bench to reach the dish of tomatoes on the windowsill. Rosie says putting tomatoes in the fridge does something inadvisable to their enzymes and stops them being tasty. These tiny cherry ones, sun-warmed, taste delicious. He pops one straight in his mouth and adds the others to his meal.

He thinks of Martin Kelly and friends – well, Friends – in the States, blending *Conservative* Quaker experience with the model of em*ergent* church, and coming up with "Convergent Quakers" as a way of describing the blending and bridging of gaps that belong to this postmodern age.

Spreading butter on his bread – not to the depth he prefers, because of his heart – Sid wonders if *Deum de Deo, Lumen de Lumine* is the sign of an emergent God. Tentatively, his mind reaches for, and touches with its fingertips, the memory of scientific articles he has read about the holographic universe – the cosmic projection of unseen Mind, the chiaroscuro of creation, lumen de lumine, projecting all three-dimensional form from its divine imagination. And he thinks about fractals. He gets up from the table for a moment, still chewing, and goes to search for Martin Buber's *Ten Rungs*, the collection of Hasidic sayings. He has turned down the corner of one page to mark a paragraph he goes back to again and again: "This is the secret of the unity of God: no matter where I take hold of a shred of it, I hold the whole of it. And since the teachings and all the commandments are radiations of his being, he who lovingly does one commandment utterly and to the core, and in this one commandment takes hold of a shred of the unity of God, holds the whole of it in his hand, and has fulfilled all."

It's hard to keep the book open and apply butter and cheese to a new piece of bread torn from the loaf. Sid hits upon the idea of holding it open with the edge of the breadboard, but not before he's transferred chutney onto the page, and smeared butter on it trying to wipe off the chutney. But he's too taken up with his train of thought to be overly irritated. That will come later – the next time he opens the book, probably.

He turns over and over in his mind the Nicene Creed's expression of the Trinity as emergent God – *Deum de Deo, Lumen de Lumine* – light fractals, divine fractals. God as Spirit in the heart of humanity, in the pulse and breath of Creation, God unfolding fractally in all that lives. God as Son, in the one who draws alongside; the Emmanuel who shares the way as Brother – as Friend. Emergent forms of God. Diverse forms of experience, Convergent into a central vital core of Reality, the Deo from which the Deum proceeds, the Lumine out of which the Lumen shines, issues forth.

He thinks of George Fox's words, beloved to all Friends: "Be patterns, be examples in all countries, places, islands, nations wherever you come; that your carriage and life may preach among all sorts of people, and to them; then you will come to walk cheerfully over the world, answering that of God in everyone; whereby in them you may be a blessing, and make the witness of God in them to bless you."

He considers the wording of it. Patterns and examples... fractals repeating... *Lumen de Lumine*. Answering that of God in everyone – the trust that in every cell of Creation the hand of the Creator may be discerned, in every soul the divine spark shines, *lumen de lumine*. "In them you may be a blessing, and make the witness of God in them to bless you." Nesting, reflecting, holographic, fractal echoings of truth and light. Godhead that goes on emerging, streaming forth, reliably creating.

The oddity of it is, Sid thinks, taking off his glasses with his left hand and rubbing an itch on his forehead with the back of his right hand, its fingers being occupied by a chunk of apple, that "clone" does not apply. Because God is *I Am That I Am*,[42] the self-originating uniqueness of the divinity means that every spark of being issuing forth in the stream of creation must be faithfully, as created, unique. Because to be a fractal of God, to replicate God, *means* being unique. They are the same inasmuch as they all bear the Light, the indelible, unmistakable mark of the divine.

He considers the Father, source of original Light, emergent as Son, as Spirit; and Father, Son and Spirit convergent as one God; creating, sustaining and redeeming in an effortless stream of life and love. He glances down again at the open book: "This is the secret of the unity of God: no matter where I take hold of a shred of it, I hold the whole of it." *Amazing*, thinks Sid. *Amazing*.

He doesn't notice the point at which the final, clear, pure tones of the *Agnus* resolve into their *dona nobis pacem*, and leave the house in a consummate fulfilment of quiet, but it occurs to him that silence has reigned now for some little while.

He hears Rosie's slow, gentle tread along the passageway, and he feels pleased to see in her face the inward smile of a Buddha as she comes into the kitchen. Music, he thinks, wakes up the soul.

She stands for a moment, surveying the table spread with his casual repast.

"That looks nice," she says. "I think I'll join you."

For sharing and wondering

- What would your "Desert Island Discs" be?
- How do you respond to the thought of God as Light? Does it feel beautiful, or impersonal, or vague, or... ?
- What images or metaphors have you found helpful in understanding the Trinity?

42 Exodus 3:14.

Into the Mystery

Lord of the Universe, yours is the only power, the only life, for you are the great I AM. Beyond our power to comprehend, infinite and marvellous, defeating our imagination, eternal and boundless. Help us, then, to make a start, to take hold of one small shred of who you are – and by so doing, take hold of all of you, forever.

22

Feast of St Julian of Norwich

"The greening of England," Rosie murmurs. Their kitchen sink is fitted just below the window looking down the garden. She stands with her hands stilled in the sudsy washing-up water, gazing at the leaves coming into full canopy on the trees, the blowing petals of blossom, the heady blue sky with its chasing clouds.

"That sounds very Shakespearean," says Sid.

"Just so. That's what I think. Every year at this time, the old country ballads come to my mind of lads and lassies a-maying, of flirtatious girls hunting vainly along the green lanes for their strayed spotted cows, of ladies dancing at Whitsun, of the cuckoos calling and the long days of the light and the green shade of the woodland. Oh, Sid! I *love* England!"

Sid smiles, coming to stand behind her, folding his arms around her. She tips her head back a little, leaning against him, and they feast their eyes on the loveliness of their garden – fruit trees, and climbing roses on the arch in full shining leaf but the buds not yet burst.

"Is it a saint's day, Sid? Is there someone who loved England – the greenwood and the hills, the pastures and the fenlands under the open sky?"

"Ah, well – as it happens! Let me come past you to fill the kettle, Rosie, and I'll tell you. It is a saint's day indeed."

He boils the kettle and spoons coffee into the cafetière. As it steams aromatically, he gets the cups and the milk, telling her: "Today, 13 May, is the day Dame Julian of Norwich recovered from a very severe illness. I guess that's why the Catholic church keeps her feast on this date. Technically she's not a saint in the church's terminology – I mean, she was never canonized. But they call her 'Blessed', and they still do keep her feast.

"It suits her that her day should fall at this time, the season of the light, because of what she was. Julian became an anchoress – do you know about anchorites?"

"Well…" Rosie frowns, thinking. "Yes. I've heard of them, though I know next to nothing about them. I've certainly heard of Dame Julian, though. She lived in the Middle Ages – and didn't she write a book?"

"She did. Not just any book – it was the earliest surviving book in the English language written by a woman. She wrote it in the second half of the fourteenth century, and then there are records of the mystic, Margery Kempe, who wrote the first autobiography we know for sure was written in England, going to visit Julian in 1413."

"How interesting! Were they different from the establishment – radicalized, I mean? Was it like a kind of early feminism?"

Sid's eyebrows rise, the thought intriguing and surprising him. "Well, I guess in a way, they were. Certainly Dame Julian's writing parried the threats and controlling credo of the church hierarchy – the terror of hell and damnation by which the people could be frightened into submission. And she spoke of Christ as our mother – that didn't go down so well at the time either. She wrote of God's tenderness and mercy, how quick he is to forgive – her book was called *Revelations of Divine Love*, and it's precisely what it says on the tin. There's a freedom in it – a trust and confidence in the love of God in Christ; nurturing, understanding. She teetered on the brink of universalism. She said there is no wrath in God; she asserted that the divine wrath we perceive has been projected there by us. 'To me was shown no harder hell than sin,' she said – and she believed that though there is a hell, behind it stands the mystery of God's love."

"And... an anchoress, you said? That's what? A monastic order?"

"Sort of. The anchorites – or anchoresses – were solitaries with a particular vocation. Like the Benedictines, they took a vow of stability, to remain in their particular location, but the anchorites kept a rather extreme form of stability, because their life was enclosed in the most literal sense. They lived in small houses called anchorages, each one built onto the outside wall of a church. One window opened into the church, through which the anchorite received the Eucharist, and the other opened onto the street. But there was no door. They didn't go out. I think it varied a bit. I've read of an anchoress with some kind of livestock – a goat or a cow – and the anchorite would have a servant fulfilling the same function as the extern sisters in an enclosed religious order, going out to get the groceries and bring in supplies. So it wasn't simply like being bricked up in a cupboard. And there was a gentleness and joy in their outlook, a love of life. Dame Julian had a cat, for example.

"Their occupation had two aspects; one was devotion, represented by the window into the church, and the other was listening and godly counsel – hearing people's troubles via the window onto the street, and offering them wisdom. There was no doubt an intercessory element, too. The space between the two windows was like the chambers of a heart beating for God, where people were prayed for, immersed in the core of the holy. Dame Julian's anchorage was pulled down by Henry VIII's reformers, but they've built something similar, to give us the idea – with a doorway in from the church so you can go inside. We could take a trip to Norfolk and see it for ourselves, if you like."

Rosie nods in assent to this possibility. "That sounds nice." She sips her coffee. "So why was it called an anchorage? Because it's anchored against the church wall?"

"Oh – no, no, no! You remember I said their occupation had the two aspects, the interior devotion and the outward ministry to ordinary people? Well, that's what they *did*, but it's not what they *were* – not their *vocation* as such. They were called anchorites – and this is the nub of their calling to stability – because their vocation was to anchor the Light to their particular local spot of Earth. That, to me, is wonderful. They gave – opened – their lives to be anchors of the Light. Sends shivers down my spine. What higher aspiration could you have on this Earth? There is something about the anchorites that does remind me of the Quakers. Julian's liberal, open theology, not shaped by fear or paranoia about heresy."

"So they were hermits? Just kind of freelance?"

"Yes, hermits of a sort. Enclosed, contemplative. But with this openness. They lived out the understanding of a God you could always come to: the God who is actually there. Mystics, but available. And they were held together as a fraternity by the *Ancrene Riwle*.[43] It's also known as the *Ancrene Wisse*. 'Wisse' is a Middle English word – comes from a German root, as in *ich weiss*, meaning 'I know'. And *Y wisse* is the Middle English for 'I know'. The German *ich wusste* means 'I realized' or 'I knew'. Obviously it's where our words 'wise' and 'wisdom' grow from. 'Ancrene Wisse' is usually translated 'Guidance for Anchoresses' – but, you know, there's a hint in the title of the respect and esteem in which they were held, because presumably you could equally well represent it as 'Anchorite Wisdom' or 'What Anchorites Know' or 'How the Anchorite Life is Realized'. 'Ancrene Wisse' is a bag that holds a lot, as titles go.

"Anyway, they lived by that and it bound them into a fraternity. It formalized the wisdom for both the outward everyday things, and their inner life focused on God. Anchoring the Light."

"So – you think this is a good time of year to remember Julian because it's a time of rising light?"

"Absolutely. And because she – brought up under the majestic Norfolk skyscape – gave up the outer freedom to go inside, forever,

---

43 Said (and means), "Ancrene Rule" – it's Middle English.

to the wide open spaces of God's love revealed in mystic union, in the secret enclosed chambers of the human heart."

For sharing and wondering

- How do you feel about solitude?
- What kind of praying do you find most helpful?
- What difference does gender make in exercising Christian ministry?

Into the Mystery

Help us to find you, secret God, in silence and solitude. Help us to share you, God with us, in loving community.

23

Ordinary Time – Life

"Sid," says Rosie, as they sit on the garden bench side by side, with their mugs of coffee, on this sweet May morning, "what do you think about suicide? And euthanasia? Do you think they are wrong?"

What Sid does think is that he had not anticipated the intellectual rigours of being married to this particular woman. Oh, she likes pretty shoes and heavenly perfume, she has an impressive collection of earrings – but nobody could call his Rosie shallow.

"I'm not an enthusiast," he answers, cautiously, "but I think it's understandable. I cannot see that any person would choose death unless their experience of life had come to feel intolerable, beyond what they could manage."

"Do you think… do you think suicide is a sin? And euthanasia?"

Sid sighs, and shifts uncomfortably. "Oh, golly. I'm not sure, to be honest Rosie, that when I think about euthanasia and suicide, sin is the first thing on my mind. Such a thing would always be personal, individual. And if I knew someone considering terminating their own life or someone else's, I think I'd have a few questions to ask about *them* before I felt eager to press my personal moral convictions upon them. Like, what was it in particular making their circumstances feel unbearable, and could I help."

"Your moral convictions, you said. So you do think there's a moral aspect to it."

"Yes. Yes, I do. It's to do with my understanding about the nature of life, and why we are here. I'm with those people who say we are spiritual beings having a physical experience, and the question is – why? I can only conclude it must be to strengthen and deepen the quality of our spiritual nature. I think we must be here to learn about love and courage, integrity and kindness, compassion. Maybe we were sent here to learn to hold our light steady amid the turbulence of the energy fields of Earth. But whyever we came here, I think there is a continuum of life. Our time here is just one section in a much longer journey. This is not all there is.

"In the learning, the developing of our spiritual nature, I believe the one thing that really counts is the choices we make. It might seem obvious to say it, but it really doesn't matter how clever or beautiful or talented or powerful we are. That is quite immaterial. What matters is what we choose to do with the possibilities life offers us – in terms of both advantages and adversity. And it's my belief that what we choose makes up the character we take with us into the life to come. Nobody can say for sure what happens after we die, but I do believe death is just a doorway through – not an ending. That can be a source of hope, but it also has other implications, mainly that the choices we made here will still follow us. Possibly also that the hard lessons we dodged and ran away from here, will still be waiting for us, compounded with the need to learn a lesson about steadfastness. Or something. That's what I think – but it's my own morality, Rosie. I wouldn't want to lay it on anyone else."

"Haven't you run away sometimes?" she asks him. "Your first marriage comes to mind. And from the Catholic church to be a Quaker. You didn't always stay with what was difficult."

"No, sure. Sometimes there's simply nothing more you can do to improve a situation; you have to just leave it and move on."

"Isn't that exactly what the people who choose to end a life are thinking too?"

"I guess they are. Yes, I guess so. But – it's a bit final, isn't it?"

"Well, is it though? If as you believe, life is part of a continuum."

Sid is silent, thinking. "I don't honestly know, Rosie. But what do you think, anyway?"

She has been drinking her coffee while she listens to him, and now she sets her empty mug down on the grass, right beside the foot of the bench where it won't get knocked over.

"Oh, I'm with you in thinking the first thing to do is to clarify the picture of the particular situation, rather than come rushing in with advice and ideological imperatives.

"Because I've worked as a care assistant with people who are dying, I've had lots of chances to watch how life ends, Sid. Where people go wrong is in assuming it just gets worse and worse and worse. It isn't like that. In life-threatening progressive illness, it can get seriously grim as you go deeper into it – no doubt about that. And what I've read of people choosing to end their life is that they assume when it gets really gritty they should bail out then before things get any tougher. But my observation is that – at least where things are handled well, I can't speak for situations where they're not – there comes a point where something changes. The last bit of life is not usually the worst bit of all. It is often characterized by a particular calm, a tranquillity, as the person lines up with death. So people choosing euthanasia or suicide get the grim bit but miss the peaceful bit. They end their lives at the worst possible moment. And I think it's a shame about that.

"Then, when people choose suicide not because they're terminally ill but because their lives have gone horrendously wrong... what I think about that again depends on the situation. I do honestly believe that if they have just gone into a school playground with an automatic weapon and taken out twenty or so little kiddies then turned the gun on themselves – well, that might actually be a wise choice. But if it's more that their money has run out and their spouse has abandoned them, and they feel lousy and frightened and see no hope for tomorrow, that's something different. In such a case, I think they need to wait and see. It really is true that the darkest hour is just before the dawn. When we reach the point we can no longer cope with the situation, that's the moment when something is about to change. And I've lived through enough terror and misery in my own life to bear testimony that out of the very circumstances that broke you up, the sweetest joys of your future will start to grow. You just have to hang in there and give it time."

Sid nods. This makes sense to him. "There's one more thing," he says. "In the Bible, in one of the letters of St Paul, he talks about being subject to the government. Well, I'm not so sure about that, being a pacifist and all; but I'm interested in the way he puts it. 'Let every soul be subject unto the higher powers,' he says. 'For there is no power but of God: the powers that be are ordained of God.'[44] I trust in God, Rosie. I don't believe he will ever let us down or let us go. I believe our times are truly in his hands. And when things get rough in my own life, I say this quietly to myself, over and over again. 'There is no power but of God.' Absolutely nothing that can ever happen to me could vanquish him. And he has my back. Which isn't the same as saying I'm never crushed by circumstances, and certainly isn't saying that I'm never afraid."

For sharing and wondering

- What is the place of law in the care of the dying?
- What are your hopes and fears, for the ending of your life?
- What have you learned from your own encounters with death?

Into the Mystery

O God our maker, our healer, our eternal home, in all our dealings with one another – from the moment of conception until the last breath – help us to remember that this is a vulnerable person, needy of tenderness, worthy of respect, made in your image and entrusted to our love.

---

44 Romans 13:1.

24

Ordinary Time – Barking Up the Wrong Tree

"Christianism," says Rosie. "Barking up the wrong tree."

"I'm sorry? What? Are you doing the crossword?" Sid looks round from the shoe he is mending, gazing at her in bewilderment over the top of the spectacles perched well down his nose.

"No," she says, "I'm not. I'm thinking about Gandhi and the Dalai Lama."

Sid absorbs this information but does not feel particularly enlightened. "OK," he says, encouragingly. He waits a moment, but nothing more seems to be forthcoming, so he goes back to what he was doing, carefully spreading the glue along the inner edge of the broken sole.

"Salvation," says Rosie. "Salvation." She nurses her coffee cup, her face brooding and dark. "A salve is what you put on a place where you've been hurt, where it's sore and stings, to soothe and heal it, to make you well again. Salvation is a good word for what Jesus does to the human soul. Salvation is the physician's work of Jesus. Nobody means to be corrupt, Sid. Nobody means to go wrong. Even those people who have shown themselves capable of the most sickeningly cruel and horrid things. Blame and condemnation are just lazy thinking. Salvation goes the long way round, to make them whole again. Not even in this life, maybe. Perhaps in some people the wiring is so badly tinkered with and messed up that they will have to go back to the maker's factory before they can be fixed. Who knows? But if salvation is worthy of its name, it's for the patient understanding with which God regards the damaged, malfunctioning soul, the wisdom with which he finds the hurt place and touches it, makes things all right again. Like Naaman,[45] you know? Whose flesh was restored from its leprosy to be like that of a little child again. Not wrinkly, not scabby, not teetering on the edge of cancer or puckered with scar tissue. A second chance.

"So I think that's what salvation is. Being made whole. And, here's what I think it's not. I think salvation is not – N O T – acquiescence. You know, like they made poor old Cranmer recant before they put him to the flames. And he did it because he hoped he might save his life. And then, when he saw that nothing would make any difference, they were going to burn him anyway, he was ashamed that he had denied his own truth. He held the hand that had signed his recantation into the fire, that it might be the first bit of him burned. Just as long as I've been going to church Sid, which is all my life, on and off, that's what they've made God out to be like. Someone who will burn you – not to death but to eternity – if you don't kowtow to the creeds of the church, and beyond that to the definitions and add-on interpretations of the church. Like, for example that 'the word of God' is synonymous with 'the Bible' – when in the scriptural record it is the preached word, the prophetic word, and the *Logos*. The pronouncing of truth that goes to the heart of a situation to bring forth life. But it's so much more convenient to have it in print, especially if you allow only your own interpretation.

"I remember once, Sid, being at a Bible study on that teaching of Jesus about the sheep and the goats.[46] How he divided them according to the way they had lived, what they had done. And the ones that had been compassionate were with him in glory, but he would not recognize the ones who had been heartless and mean.

45 2 Kings 5.
46 Matthew 25:31–46.

The person leading the study said at first glance it seemed like Jesus was saying people went to heaven because they were good. But, he said, we knew it couldn't possibly mean that; Jesus couldn't possibly have meant what he was saying because we know that the only way to get to heaven is to believe in Jesus. Therefore, he said, Jesus must have been talking about a subset of believers. First hurdle: believe in Jesus. Second hurdle: be kind and good. Then you're in.

"So I've known people who say that Gandhi and the Dalai Lama will go to hell because they weren't Christian, they didn't believe in Jesus. But that doesn't make sense to me. How could hell be hell with the Dalai Lama in it? He would change the nature of hell and make it heaven. Light cannot help dispelling darkness. That's just how it is.

"Suppose your daughter Alison went travelling in a foreign country. Imagine she went to stay with two families, and she told both of them her name was Alison and she came from England and she's thirty-four. Let's say one of the families got that right and always knew her name and how old she is and where she came from, but the other family was convinced she was called Andrea, aged thirty-eight and came from Peru. What would that matter? If both the families took her in and fed and housed her, were kind and welcoming to her, became her friends, would she feel inclined to condemn one of them to eternal damnation because they thought she was called Andrea? Good grief!

"If people call God Allah or Shiva or Vishnu, why would he mind? The Name of the Lord – that strong tower we can run into and be saved – is I Am That I Am; his *very nature*, not an epithet."

Satisfied his repair is going to hold, Sid is clearing up the spread newspaper and all the bits and pieces.

"What do you make," he asks, "of the first Christian creed – 'Jesus is Lord'?"

Rosie looks up at him. "I think it means that humanity has had a wonky handle on power. A skewed understanding of leadership.

A back-to-front take on authority. We have always seen it in terms of hierarchy and asserted it by force and punishment. The right to put someone to death, or the *droit de seigneur* men exercised over women. The power to imprison and torture, coerce and condemn. The social position that meant 'I can do this to you. And you? There ain't one solitary single thing you can to about it'. But 'Jesus is Lord' challenges all that. It says, you've got it upside-down buddy. 'Jesus is Lord' is shorthand for 'Love is stronger than fear and cruelty, truth will shine clear in the end, gentleness is the real strength, authority comes from accepting responsibility, and the most powerful thing a person can do in this world is forgive.' I tell you what 'Jesus is Lord' *doesn't* mean. It doesn't mean, 'Agree to this or I will make your life a living hell.' That's just Christianism, the brittle shell of empty religion."

"Oh," says Sid. "I... just a minute." He puts the gathered bits in his hands down on the table again and goes to the bookcase, running his finger along the row of journals and commonplace books where, over decades, he has scribbled his thoughts and hoarded quotations. "It's... yes! Here. This: 'And remember you go out not to seek man, there is no such being as Man; there are only men, each called of God, each free to obey, or refuse; each unique; you go out to seek men and you go out to bring them not Christianity, there is no such thing as Christianity, it is a word coined to deceive you; you go out to bring them Christ.' Only I don't know who said it. Silly. I never wrote it down. Elizabeth Goudge, I think, but I'm not sure.[47] It's what you meant though, isn't it?"

"Absolutely," says Rosie. "That very thing. It was always, completely, about the heart and the life, the orientation of the soul. It was always about the real thing and not just about the words."

---

47 Reader, this is actually true. It's not just Sid. Miranda, the copy-editor, has run this to ground with St Francis as the source, so I think it's probably from Elizabeth Goudge's St Francis of Assisi.

For sharing and wondering

- What does it mean to you, to say "Jesus is Lord"?
- Is it enriching to have many different religions in the world, or would it be better if we all converted to the same one? What are your feelings about diversity of religion?
- How would you describe your experience of salvation?

Into the Mystery

The world is so big, Father God, and our outlook so fearful and limited. May our confidence in you grow to a kindly generosity, firm in our faith but interested and understanding towards others.

25

Ordinary Time – Kairos

"Sid," Rosie says to her husband, "it's almost time to go. Not quite yet, but in ten minutes we will have to leave, for definite. Otherwise we'll miss the train. So if you want to go to the toilet or change your clothes, this is your moment. I'm not nagging you; just saying. I'll lock up."

Sid looks up from the letter he's writing, to smile at her. "*Kairos!*" he says.

"What?"

"Nothing. I'll tell you later. I'll just address this and seal it up, then I'm good to go."

Half an hour after that, sitting opposite each other on the London-bound train, Rosie brings her gaze back from the fields and woods clothing the gentle Sussex hills, asking: "Kairos?"

"The alternative to Chronos," says Sid.

Rosie's eyebrows are raised. Say more, her face invites.

"The two kinds of time," Sid explains. "Chronos – I'm sorry, this is obvious, but I'll say it anyway – is where the term 'chronological' originates. Chronological time is sequential time; what Mark Twain meant when he said life is just one darned thing after another.[48] It's linear time, string-of-beads time, one event succeeding another until finally you run out of time and it stops.

---

48 Although popularly attributed to Mark Twain, this may have originated either with Frank Ward O'Malley, American newspaperman, 1875–1932, or perhaps Elbert Hubbard, American writer, 1856–1916, in the form of "Life is just one damned thing after another".

"The interesting thing about it is that Chronos, one of the gods in the Greek pantheon and the personification of Time, has almost fused in mythology with the Titan called Cronos. The Titans were also deities, but ranked below the main gods. Cronos the Titan carries a sickle, and represents harvest – but he also used his sickle to castrate his father, the sky-god Uranus. And Cronos ate his children because he was jealous of them. So a mythological compound of Chronos and Cronos – the god and the Titan, with and without the 'h' – created the Father Time figure with his scythe; which, of course, is also an image of death.

"Chronological time does really consume the lives of its children. Chores, duties, hobbies, pastimes – the way we spend time, one event after another – they consume our life. And then our time is gone, and so are we. It's how our lives are eaten up.

"Kairos is different. It does mean 'time', but it also means 'action'. It's more like tim*ing*, if you see what I mean. Like an actor's cue. It's a moment that somehow stands apart from the string of one darned thing after another, and says: 'Now!' It's time in the sense of opportunity, and you have to be ready because it requires a response. Kairos timing is the heart of martial arts. In the *Tao Te Ching*, Lao Tsu says, 'In action, watch the timing.'[49] So the ancient civilizations of both West and East saw that success was absolutely contingent on the 'when' as well as the 'what'.

"A kairos moment in the Bible is when the wise men see the star appear in the East. It's what they've been watching and waiting for; when they see that star, they know it's time to go. So it's not just serendipitous, their recognition of the kairos came on the back of a lifetime of learning and studying, paying attention.

"It's a model of the prophetic life, because it's God's timing. It presumes a person living like the dog who rests with one ear cocked, one eye open and watching his master, waiting for his word. Events good or bad, or just plain ordinary, come and go like the passing

49 *Tao Te Ching*, chapter 8.

landscape seen from the window of this train. But every now and then there comes a moment with a capital M – a moment from outside the sequential flow of ordinary life; an intervention in a way, and yet belonging absolutely to this life, this person. Perhaps 'intersection' would be a better word; the instant when the path of the everyday crosses the stellar way of heaven. The chance of a lifetime."

"It sounds very exciting," says Rosie. "So, it's just one special moment – the big break your hopes and dreams have been leading up to."

"Ye-es," says Sid, "it can be. But it can also be a principle for everyday – a way to live your life. All of us are subject to chronological time, without doubt, the biological clock and the procession of events. But the *prophetic* life is attuned to kairos not to chronos – it responds to the whisper of the Spirit; its secret of effectiveness is that it gets up and goes when the Spirit says 'Now!'"

"Oh, right," says Rosie. "'If you want to go to the toilet or change your clothes, this is your moment. Otherwise we'll miss our train.' That's why you said 'Kairos'."

"Bingo," says Sid. "You got it. An interesting thing about it is that although 'kairos' is a word for a kind of time – or a way of looking at time and interacting with time, maybe – there is also a sense in which it's precisely *not* time, but a moment when the chronological procession is paused and something from outside, something divine, intervenes. The ancient Greeks thought of it as a momentary lapse of time, in which everything happens."

"Oh, wow!" says Rosie. "Wouldn't that be the same as Eternal Life? You know how people make a word play on 'the present' and say the secret of life is to receive 'the present', God's gift; unwrap it. Remember how Jesus said we would never be able to enter the Kingdom of Heaven unless we change and become like little children?[50] Children live in the present moment, don't they? They can only thrive on spontaneity. Maybe we were born to live by the kairos, and the chronos is like an illness, an acquired oppression."

50 Matthew 18:3.

Sid smiles. "It has been said. But I think, in all honesty and for practical purposes, the two have to work together. You have to get up and go or you'll miss your train – that's the kairos; but if anything was typified by chronos it must surely be a railway timetable. A spiritual being in an earthly situation – which is what we are – has to manage the delicate art of balancing both. It's about being appropriate, and about being inspired."

"Tunbridge Wells!" says Rosie. "Jeepers, that was quick – look – here we are, Sid; this is our stop!"

For sharing and wondering

- Do you like to just eat when you're hungry, or do you prefer to follow regular meal times?

- To what extent do schedules (whether your own, or those of others) determine the patterns of your life in general? Has this varied from time to time – at school, caring for a young family, in employment or self-employment, on retirement? How much is this a matter of your choice?

- Can you think of a kairos moment in your own life – a tide you had to take or else lose the opportunity?

Into the Mystery

Help us, God of hope and life, to see the opportunities held out to us in every day. Give us the grace to travel light and with curiosity, to make the most of life's richness and wonder. Free us from timidity and mindless repetition, to celebrate this magnificence, that we are gloriously alive.

26

Ordinary Time – Why Sid Became a Quaker

"Why did you become a Quaker, Sid?"

Rosie takes up the twigs of thyme she has gathered from the garden. She strips off the little leaves with a practised hand, into the silky flour mounded in the bread bowl in front of her. She glances up at him, questioningly, as she reaches for the box of sea salt flakes. He has heard. He's thinking.

Rosie and Sid have not been married all that long, their life paths wending through all manner of experiences and adversities before they intertwined. A lack of shared history means that even now, after eight years together, there are still things she feels surely she should know by now – but doesn't.

She pours in a stream of green-amber olive oil, then the gently warm water. Yeast is in already, and the brown sugar to feed it.

"I… it was because… er… " Sid is floundering. Oh, he knows why his feet found their way to the Friends Meeting House, but it's not so easy to put it into words.

Rosie has mixed her bread batter and turns it out onto the floured tabletop. She begins to knead. Sid sighs.

"Don't say if you don't want," says Rosie quickly. But he does want this. He wants her to know him.

"It was because," he says, hesitantly, "Jesus is the way and the truth and the life."

Rosie frowns, puzzled. "That's a reason to become a Christian," she says, "not a Quaker in particular."

"I used to find," Sid explains, "that all the doctrine got in the way. Any statement of faith leads inexorably to some kind of inquisition. Right at the beginning, before the church formally existed, there were the people Jesus had touched and loved and healed. He asked a lot of them, from what I've read. He said you couldn't be his disciple – couldn't follow him, couldn't learn from him – unless you gave up everything you had.[51] That's... well... jeepers!"

He shakes his head in wonder at the cost of discipleship.

"So I think," he goes on, "it's like it says in the Quaker *Advices and Queries* – that Christianity is not a notion, but a way. It's about how you live. But as time went on, things got formalized, creeds were developed and agreed on. In the early days the people who loved Jesus, and wanted to be part of what he stood for, met to break bread and to pray, and they were amazed to find and touch again the living Jesus in their midst – opening the Scriptures to them, warming their hearts, kindling hope again. And over time that got formalized too, into the Eucharist – the Mass.

"Creeds unite people of course, and sacraments do too. But the danger is always of uniting around the thing, not the one who inspired it. And then again, once you have a creed you have a who's-in-who's-out situation. It unites, yes – but it excludes too. You have a sacrament, then next thing you know, you have compulsory attendance at Mass, obligatory confession, certificates of baptism, social ostracizing of couples who aren't married and their children born out of wedlock. It's not a far jump from there to burning people alive or disemboweling them for not acquiescing to your creed.

"I guess... well, the honest truth is, I got really turned off by the church's preoccupation with doctrine. Arguing. Who believes in the physical resurrection and who doesn't. Or the virgin birth of Jesus. Or whether women can be priests. Or whether the Bible is

51 Luke 14:33.

infallible – or the Pope, or the dogma of the church. I saw people speak with complacency about folk burning in eternal hell fire for not acquiescing to this or that doctrine. I saw church people split and divide and turn their backs on each other over this or that difference of opinion. And in the end, I had to conclude this was not for me.

"But that didn't let me off being part of the people of God. And I was hooked on Jesus. I love Jesus. I belong to him. I'm his property – all of me. So for a while I was just stumped. What to do?

"And that was when I came across the Society of Friends. I read about George Fox saying that Christ came to teach his people himself, and something in me really responded to that, especially when I put it together with the Quaker idea of Christianity being not a notion but a way. It seemed to me that the key to the thing lay in having a living relationship with a living Christ – communion not as an enacted rite but actual and personal. And no vicar – in fact nothing vicarious at all – but a direct, intimate, first-hand experience and knowledge."

Sid stops and thinks, then he begins to laugh. Rosie, her kneading almost finished, lifts her eyes from what she is doing to look at him, brows questioningly raised.

"Well," he says, "if I thought they argue in regular church, I tell you nothing could have prepared me for the Quakers and their verbal boxing matches! They may meet for worship in silence but, by heck, can they argue!

"And one of the things they discuss is how Christian they are or aren't. I've listened to all manner of harangues starting 'Surely we can all agree…' and 'What we should all believe…' But the beauty of it is, though there's surely space for the liveliest debate, the bottom line is still that Friends believe Christianity is not a notion but a way. You can't organize around a way like you can round a creed or a sacrament, because the thing about a way is that it won't stand still. It develops. It travels. It moves on. The landscape changes, it isn't static. A way won't permit you to exclude or excommunicate like a notion will.

"So, I come into meeting on a Sunday morning, into the silence and the Light, having in mind the words of George Fox: 'Why should any man have power over any other man's faith, seeing Christ himself is the author of it?' I am there as no one's inquisitor. When I sit in meeting, opening my heart to the Light, I trust the Christ who came to teach his people himself to find me and meet with me, and what his business and his relationship is with the Friend who sits next to me is not mine to enquire and beyond me to understand. It is more wisely explored in the silence than examined by a creed.

"I guess what I'm saying, Rosie, is that I found the Friends more accepting. I became a Quaker because I don't like shutting people out or drawing lines in the sand to create divisions. I believe in the divine spark in every heart – what Fox called 'that of God in every man'. It's an optimistic faith, and humble – and that suits me well."

Rosie nods, spreading oil over the beautiful cushion of dough, covering it with a damp cloth as she returns it to the bread bowl and sets it to rise.

"Makes sense to me," she says.

For sharing and wondering

- Where did you first go to church and with whom?
- How did you come to choose the church community in which you now worship? If you don't go to church, what sort of worshipping community would appeal to you?
- What aspects of Christian faith do you find especially challenging or puzzling?

Into the Mystery

Jesus… Lord and Master, Friend and Brother, thank you for taking care of us, understanding and loving us, shining your light for us to find the way. Help us to take you seriously, to be faithful in what you ask of us, and to live in such ways as you can be proud of.

27

Corpus Christi

"Nothing happens after Trinity Sunday for ages and ages, does it Sid? It goes: Easter, Ascension, Pentecost, Trinity – then Sundays after Trinity like something falling down the stairs, hitting one step after another until it finally hits the ground at Harvest Festival. That is to say, I suppose there are loads of saints' days – I mean there isn't one day of the year without at least one saint's day on it, is there? But the more you have the less they mean. There isn't really anything special between Trinity Sunday and Harvest Festival – is there?"

"Oh my goodness, there certainly is!" Galvanized into an emphatic response by his astonishment at this lamentable ignorance, Sid beholds his wife, amazed. She giggles at his shocked face. "Sorry, Sid! Go on, then – tell me."

"Well, there's the Summer Solstice, and Lammas; there's St Benedict's Day and St Clare of Assisi; and this Thursday is Corpus Christi. You – surely you've heard of Corpus Christi?"

"A Catholic feast, presumably – seeing it's in Latin and nobody's heard of it?"

"Ouch! That's a bit harsh! Catholic in the true sense, maybe – as in, universal, the full glory of the church militant here on Earth. But, Corpus Christi – it's a corker of a feast is that; not something to be ignored or belittled; no siree!"

"Enlighten me, O wise one."

"Ha! 'Are you sitting comfortably? Then I'll begin.'[52] Corpus Christi is the core and the foundation of what the church is all about. It's where it began, it's the source of its life, and it's what's left once you take away all the buildings and committees, the robes and the choirs, the flower arrangements, the sound systems and the fights. It means – I apologize if you know this already – 'the body of Christ'.

"Generally speaking it's thought of as all about the real presence of Christ in the Eucharist. It sometimes touches on the institution of the Eucharist, but of course that's really what Holy Thursday focuses on – the Last Supper – along with Gethsemane and washing the disciples' feet. But because of the Agony in the Garden, Holy Thursday is a sombre time, almost grim; sorrow and betrayal and inescapable suffering. Corpus Christi isn't like that – it's a glorious, joyous feast. A happy feast. Processions and singing, taking to the streets with a socking great monstrance and a choir belting out *Tantum Ergo* and *Panis Angelicus*."

"What I said –" she is teasing him – "a very Roman Catholic affair."

"It doesn't stop there, though, Rosie. Yes, the body of Christ is a Eucharistic and sacramental thing, but that doesn't necessarily mean it's solely a liturgical phenomenon, or imprisoned within the dogma of any establishment.

"In the last few chapters of John's Gospel, there's the story of Doubting Thomas[53] – how the friends of Jesus had begun to meet together, and Thomas didn't turn up, so he wasn't there when Jesus came in and stood among them even though the doors were locked. He missed him! And it seemed like a cock-and-bull tale to Thomas. Jesus there with them – yeah, right! How could that be true? This was Thomas who loved Jesus so much he had been ready to stand up for him even if that meant dying with him. They gave him the epithet 'the Twin', you know – Thomas. And in South India, there's

52 These were always the opening words to the story on *Listen with Mother*, a BBC radio slot for the under-fives, broadcast every weekday. It ran from 1950 to 1982.
53 John 20.

a whole bunch of churches that sprang up quite separately from any others, which are said to have been started by Thomas himself. And in those churches, they say Thomas was *Jesus'* twin! There's a thought to conjure with! Anyway, I digress.

"John – in his Gospel – writing later than the other evangelists, was helping the church find a way to understand what their community meant now the physical presence of Jesus was no longer in their midst. And he set out to show them how, though Jesus might physically have left their company, he certainly hadn't gone; he was really and truly still with them. And John wants them to understand that they encounter the real presence of Jesus when they meet to break bread and pray. He is there in the community of the faithful. So he tells this story of how the disciples were regularly meeting, and because Thomas didn't show up, he missed out on the encounter with Jesus; when he bothered to attend the next meeting, he saw the risen Lord. What John is saying, is that where Christ is present on Earth now, is in the gathering of the faithful. The body of Christ is there – where his people are met."

"You mean – John just invented it to make a point?"

"No, I don't think so. Why would he have needed to? All he had to do was recount events in such a way that their significance came to the fore.

"Not only that, but if you look at the Last Supper itself, you have Jesus breaking the bread and saying, 'This is my body.'[54] Never has the word 'this' been so hotly debated! What did he mean? Some theologians think he meant the bread, and that in the Eucharist the presence of Christ is there in the consecrated bread, that the Communion consists of eating the bread – taking into one's very core the holy presence of Christ. But other theologians say there's more to it than that. They say that 'this' means not just the bread, but also the gathering, the breaking and the sharing – so the real presence of Christ is diffused through the community as it breaks

54 See Luke 22 and Matthew 26.

bread together. It isn't just the elements. The body of Christ is the people united in the humility of receiving this broken bread, the emblem of their ordinary everyday life.

"And of course, Quakers say it spreads out way beyond that to the whole of life. 'Eucharist' means 'thanksgiving', of course; and the early Friends believed that 'eucharist' occurred in every moment where life was kissed by the holy. George Fox and his Friends believed everything you did, every relationship, could be sacramental – a touching place with the immanent transcendent, the Mystery of life. They felt, I think, that liturgical signs and symbols have a way of freezing the life out of what is real. Like it can be said that a stuffed fox in a taxidermist's shop window is 'a real fox'. So it may be, but it ain't the same as the dancing, wary, shy, alert, wild creature that slips into the garden at dusk, or sits to sniff at a meadow flower on a summer's day. Fox – George Fox, I mean, not the one in our garden or the taxidermist's shop – thought the encounter with the holy could not be formalized in that way. I guess, for him, what Quakers call 'a gathered meeting' must have come nearest to being Corpus Christi. When the whole becomes subtly more than the sum of its parts, and the Holy Spirit is tangibly there in the midst."

"Sid Ashley, I'd put money on you being the only Quaker in Great Britain who feels moved to celebrate the feast of Corpus Christi!"

Sid smiles. "I think you may be right, there. But if you do what Quakers have sometimes called 'going beyond' – that's to say if you look for the meaning that underlies, stands behind, a teaching of the church – why there is often a greater commonality than you ever imagined. And then of course there was St Augustine, teaching his catechumens about the moment when the host was held out to them with the words 'The Body of Christ', to which they must respond 'Amen.' He said to them, 'Let your *Amen* be for *I Am*.' And 'I Am' is the name of God, and means also 'Yes, me.' Oh, it's *huge*, Rosie! Corpus Christi is a *wonderful* feast. Its resonances are immense. Once you put it all together, it's a celebration and exposition of communion – both the most intimate encounter with the secret inexpressible heart of the divine, and the most generous gathering in of the people of God."

For sharing and wondering

- What place does the Eucharist have in your life?
- Where and how does the church feel like "the body of Christ" to you?
- In what ways do you feel you could deepen your own sense of being part of the body of Christ?

Into the Mystery

Christ has no body but yours,
No hands, no feet on earth but yours,
Yours are the eyes with which he looks
Compassion on this world,
Yours are the feet with which he walks to do good,
Yours are the hands, with which he blesses all the world.
Yours are the hands, yours are the feet,
Yours are the eyes, you are his body.
Christ has no body now but yours,
No hands, no feet on earth but yours,
Yours are the eyes with which he looks
compassion on this world.
Christ has no body now on earth but yours.

St Teresa of Ávila (1515–82)

28

Birth of St John the Baptist

"It's a funny thing about the summer," says Rosie, as she stands waiting for their mugs of tea to brew. "It's like an undercooked cake. The edges are fine, but it sinks in the middle. There's often a heat wave in May – sometimes even in April. Then it slumps again in what's supposedly high summer. Like now. It's June, but it's chilly enough for a cardigan. July is often indifferent and August wet, but it's nearly always sunny in September. If I ever want to go away for a few days, I make it September, because the weather's generally nice then.

"There you go," she adds, setting Sid's tea down by the bowl of cereal he's eating.

"Thank you." He smiles at her. "Yes, Dick Smith says the one day in the year that's almost always fine is the 15th September. He says if you have a special event where it absolutely mustn't rain – a garden hand-fasting or something – then 15th September is the day to do it."

"Really?" Rosie reaches for the muesli. "That's worth remembering. I'll stash that away in my mental filing system. Who's Dick Smith?"

"That ex-policeman in Kent who predicts the weather without modern technology, using the old ways he learned from the medieval monastic records at Canterbury."

"You mean David King?"

"Yes, him. His name's got its roots wound round Dick King-Smith who writes the children's stories, in my mind. I always get them muddled."

"Oh, right. Sheep-pigs, wind days and perigees – what's the difference? So if September is the finest time of year, what's with calling June high summer? Just because it bisects the twelve-month?"

"Well…" Sid pushes his now empty cereal bowl away from him and picks up his mug, blows on his tea to cool it, takes an experimental sip. It's still too hot. He puts it down. "I think our mindset has shifted a bit since we lost sight of the agricultural year. You want dry weather for the harvest; it's crucial. September is when you need it dry. It just works that way, anyhow. The long, hot dry spell ripens and dries off the grain, finishes the tree fruit nicely, after the rains of late spring and early summer have plumped them in their growing season. With the electronic revolution and urbanization of human society, we've started to see the outdoors as a sort of playground – a leisure park for walks and picnics and fêtes and garden parties. Our view of life has become very humanocentric. The weather forecasters on the telly say if it's going to be 'nice' or not. If it rains, it'll be 'horrible' or 'nasty'. Gee! Tell that to a farmer in Burkina Faso. 'Beautiful rain', they say in Africa.

"But high summer is about the turning of the year and the seasons of the light, not the weather. The 21 June is the summer solstice – 'Litha' in the old Celtic system, one of the quarter days. For the pagans, it was the time when the goddess was great with child – heavy with the crops of the harvests to come – and the god was at the peak of his virility. It's about the Earth and the sun, their relationship. But exactly because it's the zenith of the year, there's a whisper of the darkness. From this day on, the year begins to wane. Those old pagans said the oak king, for all his glorious abundance, now surrendered to his twin brother the holly king. At Litha, in the traditional celebrations they'd light tar barrels or straw-bound wheels and roll them flaming down the hillsides. It was about the year's wheel turning, on the brink of its wane towards the darkness. Parties, huge bonfires, all-night vigils – it was a big festival."

Rosie listens to him as she eats her muesli and drinks her tea. "What did the Irish missionaries make of that? Is there a midsummer Christian feast?"

"Oh, yes – a very important one. The birth of John the Baptist. Most of the saints' days commemorate the death of the saint – because the high point of their lives is the day they enter heaven; so this is an exception, and that of itself is meant to flag up that this is something special. St John's Tide balances Christmas. They say that the birth of St John celebration is set at midsummer because St John was born six months before Jesus and the feast of his birth is midwinter – but that's a cobbled-together explanation from commentators who have lost touch with the ancient ways. That's not the reason for the timing.

"St John the Baptist is the herald. His task is to pave the way for the coming of Jesus. As St John – the Evangelist, not the Baptist – puts it: 'He was not that Light, but was sent to bear witness of that Light.'[55] That means there's an interesting thing going on where the true light – Jesus – appears in the year's darkness. So the light of summer, around which religion has centred until now, the sun-god, is not the true light but only bears witness to it. It's a redirecting of attention. St John points away from himself at high summer, to the Christ, saying 'Look! There is the true Light.'

"And, you see, 'Behold, the Lamb of God'[56] is the utterance of John the Baptist's whole life. He came to call the people to repentance. 'Repent' is a poor translation of the Greek *metanoia*, which doesn't mean 'be sorry' as 'repentance' does, but means 'turning around'. So just as Yul is the turn of the winter, Litha is the turn of the summer. And the first missionaries set the Incarnation at the winter turn, the coming of the infant light into darkness, turning the fortunes of us who were lost, by its grace; and they set St John's Tide on the summer turn because St John is the one who came preaching

55 John 1:8.
56 John 1:29.

metanoia, turning in the sense of conversion of life.

"It's the feast of his birth not his death, because midsummer is the first hint of change. It's all light and everything is lovely, but at the peak of it comes the first breath of its opposite; now comes the turning of the year. It's a balancing, and a balancing is always a reckoning, a judgment. At the height of the bright, long days of summer, we remember that nothing is permanent, that everything must die."

"The lily is in the compost," says Rosie, "and the compost is in the lily. That's what Thich Nhat Hanh says.[57] In each experience, its opposite is to be found. That's the meaning of the yin and yang symbol of Taoism, isn't it? The one like two little fishes – the black fish with the white eye and the white fish with the black eye. It's about natural balancing. Everything contains the seed of its opposite. Inherent in every birth is mortality; that is its nature.

"Anyway," she says, reaching across for Sid's bowl and beginning to stack the crockery to start the washing up: "I can see, when you put it like that, there's more to midsummer than the weather!"

She bends and kisses the top of his head before she turns to the sink with the dishes.

"You were born out of time, Sid Ashley. You should have been a medieval monk."

"You think so? I'm not so sure about that. I can think of one or two moments I might have missed if that's the way things had fallen out."

For sharing and wondering

- Describe a memory from your childhood of a summer day.
- Think of an example of repentance from your own life.
- Think of an example from your life of "the lily in the compost and the compost in the lily" – a time when, out of an experience of sadness and loss, something new and hopeful grew.

57 Revered Zen master.

Into the Mystery

From your loving hands, O God, we receive the blessing of life with all its chances and changes. Help us to travel hopefully, to trust in your goodness when the dark time comes, and to remember that everything passes.

29

Ordinary Time – Abiding Joy

When Sid comes into the living room to find Rosie lying on her back, her knees drawn up, staring blankly at the ceiling, his whole body tenses. Is she all right? Has she fallen into one of her existential black holes? Rosie walks along the cliff edge of suicidal despair too much of the time, gazing down ravenously at the far below ocean, with its rocks and pounding waves.

"Rosie?" he enquires, tentatively. "Are you OK?"

She turns her head, and her gaze meets his.

"Yes," she says. "I'm thinking about abiding joy."

Ah. Right. Not any form of annihilation, then. Not today. He sits down on the sofa. "Tell me more?"

"Well, I was reading the Bible," she says, "because I had these words in my head, and I couldn't remember where they came from. I thought it was one of the Church of England collects. I kept thinking, '… that their joy may be full' – but I couldn't remember – and then I got it. Aha! It was Jesus! He said it, in that long prayer and discourse the last night before he was arrested – the one that goes on and on in John 15, 16, 17. That one. So I looked it up. And it was really interesting. Gosh, Sid, I had such a complex of thoughts I hardly know how to untangle them to tell you. I think I'll just say it in the order I thought it.

"When my children were small, bedtime was at six, and every day had a dip between four o'clock tea and six o'clock bath and bed, when basically my energy had run out and theirs hadn't but they were getting a bit wild and incoherent. I *always* got cross. I couldn't think why my patience wouldn't stretch. And then I figured it out. As my energy ran out, I reached for more, and the only source I had was adrenalin. 'Flight' wasn't an option: I was dredging up 'fight'. Getting cross kept me going, stopped me crashing. I prayed about it, Sid, and I remember seeing that the energy of Jesus was his abiding joy. He ran on joy like cars ran on petrol and tired mothers run on adrenalin. I didn't know how to get to the place where I could do the same, but at least I'd had the insight; that was what he did.

"Gandhi – another great soul with stamina – also tapped into abiding joy. He had a mantra ('Rama... rama... rama...') that he kept running inside his mind all the time – and it's the formula for abiding joy. In Hinduism, I mean. It kept him going.

"So anyway, I had these words scrolling in my mind, 'that their joy may be full', and I realized that Jesus had *specifically prayed* for us his followers to have the same fuel he had – abiding joy.

"I went to look it up in the Bible – it's in John 15. It doesn't come until verse 11. What it says, is 'These things have I spoken unto you, that my joy might remain in you, and that your joy might be full.'

"And when I read it, I had this surge of excitement. He was saying the abiding joy that was his actual basic fuel could be *permanently* in me and *constantly* topped up! Oh, Jesus! I mean, how fab is that? It made me feel... *greedy*. Voracious. Like, I *want* that joy! *Zeloo* – you know, that Greek word – St Paul wrote to be ambitious for the higher gifts, covet them, '*zeloo* after prophecy'.[58] Well, I *zeloo* after abiding joy.

"But I noticed he said '*These things have I spoken unto you*, that my joy might remain in you'. That meant I had to read the bit before, which would be the key to getting his joy loose inside me on a permanent basis.

58   1 Corinthians 14:39.

"So I went back to the beginning of the chapter, and it's all about how Jesus is the vine and we are the branches. And he says, that we have to abide in him. That unless we do, we can do *nothing* – now that I can certainly believe!

"But he says something else I'd never noticed before. Sid, he says…" She rolls over and reaches for the open Bible lying near her on the floor, picks it up and peers at it, tracing through with her finger for the place. "He says – listen – 'every branch that beareth fruit, he purgeth it, that it may bring forth more fruit.'[59]

"And I thought about de-toxing and de-cluttering – about how much energy and lightness comes from that. It made me see that just as a person needs a clean, spacious, peaceful home to live an orderly life, and a de-toxed body, not all mucked up with sugar and booze and poisons, to be healthy, so it's important to do something similar with my actual soul – my spirit. It's what John Wesley said, cleanliness is next to godliness; they are associated. Holiness and de-toxing and de-cluttering are connected. Purging. You have to purge all the dross and rubbish for your light to shine bright."

John Wesley, eh? Sid never knew that. He constantly marvels at the bits and pieces Rosie has managed to glean on her pilgrimage through Christian denominations and world religions. So that saying, "Cleanliness is next to godliness", came from John Wesley. Well, who knew? Rosie is still talking. He tunes back in.

"Then he gives the key to the de-tox. Listen! He says: 'Now ye are clean through the word which I have spoken unto you.'[60] That means – it must do – that the words of Jesus work powerfully in us, if we take them in: 'read, mark learn and inwardly digest',[61] like Thomas Cranmer says. Powerful words. Like swallowing mashed raw garlic in castor oil disinfects the gut or administering coffee enemas makes the liver dump its toxic load. Digesting the words of Jesus cleans out

59 John 15:2.
60 John 15:3.
61 Book of Common Prayer 1549, Collect for The Second Sunday in Advent.

the soul, so that his abiding joy can flower and expand inside us, like a firework, a fountain of eternal life. Do you see?"

Sid is not sure that he does see. His mind is still recoiling from the notion of swallowing minced up raw garlic in *castor oil*, let alone how a person might go about ingesting words. But he knows it feels good to see Rosie alight and eager. And he likes the way the phrase "abiding joy" is somehow settling in his mind with something of the beautiful radiance of its meaning.

For sharing and wondering

- What are the sources of energy you turn to, when you are tired but you just have to keep going?
- Think of an area of your life that could benefit from a de-tox or de-clutter.
- Describe an experience of joy from your own life.

Into the Mystery

Help us, O God, to make room in our souls for joy. Open our eyes and ears to where joy is all around us – in music and art, in nature, in friendship and family life. Thank you, generous God, that life, if we let it be, is absolutely overflowing with joy.

30

Ordinary Time – *Ma*

"*Ma*," says Rosie.

Silence. *What?* thinks Sid.

"Er... woof?" he says. "Moo? Miaow?"

"No," she says. "*Ma*."

"My Ma? Your Ma? Grandma?"

"Nope. Just, *ma*."

"Rosie, you're going to have to explain."

She grins at him. "It's Japanese. In fact, some of the best words in the whole human community are Japanese, and this is one of them. This is the language that gave us *komorebi*, which means the interplay of light filtering through the moving leaf canopy of a tree; and *shibui*, an adjective describing a particular kind of simple, subtle, unobtrusive beauty. It relates to the noun *shibusa*, which is... er... the way something looks – its appearance; an unassuming simplicity within which complexity and sophistication are modestly hidden. In fact, simplicity and modesty are two key elements of *shibusa*. There are more. *Shibusa* is silent, implicit, ordinary – everyday – natural, and not perfect. It has restraint, a kind of rough, earthy quality, and this creates an atmosphere of sacred peace.

"Then there's *iki* – which can refer to things or situations, but is also a human characteristic – calm, simple, candid directness. Originality. Spontaneity. Audacity, even. Exquisite.

"Ooh – and *kanketsu*, the idea that the journey to simplicity can be complicated – complex. The Japanese! How do they know? What is it about their minds that leads them to consider the origins of subtlety, modesty and beauty? Then there's *wabi-sabi*, which I think I've already told you about – but you could fill a library with the books written about *wabi-sabi*!"

Sid originally came into the room to tell Rosie he was on his way out to buy a couple of cans of wood preservative for the deck in the garden, to protect it against the winter rains to come. He manages to hang onto this thought, and his accompanying errand of checking whether Rosie would like him to pick up any groceries as he's passing, but now he wants to know: "And *ma*? What does *ma* mean, then?"

"Ah! Nothing is beautiful, nothing is useful or calm or peaceful without *ma*. No work is sound without *ma*. No artistic creation can ever succeed without *ma*. No life gets far without crashing unless it has *ma*. No –"

"Rosie! Darling, I'm sorry to interrupt you. I should have said. I'm just on my way up to the hardware store for some deck stain, and I wondered if you need me to get anything. The store closes soon, so I truly must get on my way. Is there a quick definition of *ma*, or should this wait until I come home?"

Rosie looks at him. "It should wait," she says. "Because *ma* is important and cannot be rushed or compressed. You go get the wood stuff. When you come in, I'll make us some tea and tell you all about *ma*. We are low on milk but we've enough to get by. More to the point, you have no more cookies. You might like to think about that. Sid – I'll see you later."

All the way to the store and all the way home, Sid is wondering about *ma*. He has not the faintest clue what it can possibly be. Cookies do make long listening easier as an exercise, so he swings by the bakers and snags a large bag to take home. He dumps the heavy tins of preservative down in the tool shed, and strides up the garden. "Honey, I'm back!" he calls, standing still, detecting where she might be.

"In the sitting room," she calls back. "I saw you parking. I've made your tea. Put your cookies on a beautiful plate, don't eat them out of the bag."

Sid senses the influence of Japan in this last remark. Since when did Rosie care about eating food straight from the bag? She can't be bothered to peel vegetables or cut the tails and leaf-stalky bits off radishes. She tears bread, never cuts it. This is Japan speaking, not his Rosie. But he carefully selects a large white plate and places two cookies, one on top of the other, in the exact centre, as he imagines a Japanese tea-master might do.

"That's the idea," says Rosie approvingly, glancing at his cookie plate as he joins her and settles himself into his armchair.

"Now, *ma*," she says once she's poured his tea, "is the emptiness that lies between things – the intervening contextual space giving meaning to what is there. In his most excellent book of wisdom, the *Tao Te Ching*, Lao Tsu said that even though lots of spokes join up to the hub of the wheel, it's the hole for the axle in the middle that makes it any use.[62] He said that although you need porcelain clay to make a teacup, it's no darned use without the hole in the middle to pour the tea in. And he said if you build a house but you omit doors to come in and windows to look out and a big space right smack dab in the middle to actually live in, it's of no use at all. So, he said, there's profit in what *is* there but the usefulness is in what's *not* there. And the space that makes things useful and meaningful is the *ma*.

"You can have *ma* in a room – a single rose in a vase against a white wall. An earthenware bowl of peaches on a scrubbed kitchen table. A hearth swept clean so your eye is drawn to the flames of the fire. *Ma* is about not prioritizing tangible, visible, concrete things – leaving space in which they may acquire meaning and express beauty. In a cluttered room, the *ma* is all lost and everything looks like rubbish. *Ma* matters in any picture or design – the spacing, letting a shape breathe and be seen. Elegance comes from this, and stylistic beauty.

62 *Tao Te Ching*, chapter 11.

"But, look; you can also remember the *ma* in a diet – don't cram, don't be greedy, leave some space and time between mouthfuls, between courses and meals; *ma* is the antithesis of the cruise diet. A beautifully conceived cup, full of fragrant jasmine tea, steam leisurely floating and curling from it in a quiet room.

"And, you can have *ma* in a person's life – their schedule. Quiet time. A half-hour as the day begins, to pray and watch the sun rise and remember who you really are. Commitments spaced so there is time to prepare and debrief; not a hectic scramble of rush and tear, always late, fuming in traffic, irritable with everyone. In a person's life, *ma* is the art of simplicity and the habit of quietness. Jesus knew about *ma*. He took time to sit by the lakeside, and walk in the hills. It's what made his time in all the press and throng of people so absolutely useful. He brought them peace."

Sid hopes Rosie didn't want a cookie because he's just eaten the second one. Her tea's gone cold. He thinks that might be the downside of not prioritizing the tangible.

For sharing and wondering

- Imagine you have the chance to build a garden room for prayer and being peaceful. Describe it.

- Thinking of your daily life, what is the balance of priorities between the tangible and the intangible – in your home, in your schedule, in your activities? Are there any changes you would like to make?

- Where can you see the concept of *ma* in the life of Jesus?

Into the Mystery

In your presence is peace, Father. The word of your Spirit brings peace. Jesus speaks peace to nature where it is tormented or disordered. For our time and our life circumstances, grant us the privilege of become a conduit of your beautiful peace. Make us, O Lord, a channel of your peace in our day.

31

Ordinary Time – The Formless

"You're looking thinner," says Sid to Rosie, looking up from his breakfast as she wanders vaguely through the kitchen in search of a ballpoint pen to make her shopping list.

"Have you lost some weight?"

"Maybe a pound or two," Rosie offers in reluctant tones. She doesn't like to admit to ground gained because she always fears ground lost.

Sid smiles encouragingly. "Well, you're looking great! And every morning I hear your feet – pad, pad, pad – behind the closed door of the living room, and I think to myself, 'There she goes, running round her Wii Fit island!' Sometimes I wonder, where are you running to today, Rosie?"

Rosie has forgotten why she came into the kitchen, now. A familiar frustration of growing older. She looks at Sid, thoughtfully, places her hands on the back of the chair opposite where he sits. It's true she is thinner. The wedding ring on her hand resting on the chairback used to be bedded firmly in a waist formed in her flesh. It sits at a slant now, loose.

"It's always the same, Sid," she answers him. "Every day. I am running away."

Sid doesn't like the sound of this. He puts down his spoon. When Rosie says things of this nature it gives him that bad feeling in the pit of his stomach. That *Oh, here we go, Sid,* feeling.

"From what?" he asks her, cautiously.

Her eyes contemplate him, then her gaze shifts, and she looks beyond him. The window behind his chair faces east and, from the patch of sky it offers as a view, glory streams, muddling with the tossing clouds of this turbulent morning. She sighs, and shifts restlessly, frowns as if she is searching for words or can hardly be bothered to say this. Sid is afraid. Is she leaving him?

"I am running away from this Earth," she says, "a pound at a time. Pounding away! Running, running – away from the solid heavy presence I was. Running away from here. Running away from form into formlessness. *Gate, gate; paragate; parasamgate; bodhi svaha!*"

"Right," says Sid, slowly. "Er… what did you say?"

She smiles. "It's Sanskrit. Words from old India. It means, 'Gone, gone; gone beyond; absolutely gone beyond; enlightenment, brilliant, amen!' It's to do with understanding – embracing, accepting, celebrating – the impermanence of all form and being. Everything is passing, Sid, but nothing is lost. In a hundred years, this dear body of yours, and my body, they will be nothing but dust; but neither you, nor I, nor our love, will be wasted or lost. We will have passed from form into formlessness, we will be truly one because we will have gone home into the infinite."

He's a bit out of his depth with Sanskrit. Sid is a Quaker, but not your modern Quaker. He's a conservative Quaker. John Woolman and Robert Barclay, George Fox and William Penn and the holy Bible are stacked with his *Quaker Faith and Practice* by his bedside reading lamp. Sid believes Christ came to teach his people himself – and does so, and stands knocking at the door of every soul, waiting to be invited in. Sid thinks the Light is the first word of God, hatched by the Holy Spirit. He has little truck with any new-agey blend of social conscience and half-baked philosophy. Passing from form to formlessness – what? If this is just a fancy way of saying "losing weight", well and good; but… what? Is she talking about dying, or slimming, or… ?

But Sid is well-equipped for confusion and incomprehension. The Society of Friends has both a Simplicity Testimony and a Truth Testimony.[63] This means that built into their daily practice is a steady walking away from the world of multiplicity and complexity, all things labyrinthine and abstruse (the world of form), towards unadornment and openness (formlessness). So candour is natural to Friends, and thus he doesn't tie himself in internal knots but asks, "Rosie, what are you talking about?"

Rosie pulls the chair out from under the table, and sits down opposite him, her face serious – almost ferociously so.

"What I'm saying," she explains, speaking slowly as she searches for the right words, "is the Bible thing – 'He must increase and I must decrease' – what John the Baptist said about Jesus.[64] I'm trying to get inside Jesus, Sid. I want to be less tip and more iceberg. I think… I think things are coming to an end. I think the Rapture has begun. Some of the other animals are slipping away ahead of us. The Tasmanian wolf, the golden toad, the Bali tiger, the Western black rhinoceros, the Cayman thrush, the Pyrenean ibex to name just the few I can call to mind – and so many more are slipping through the door before our eyes: the giant panda, the mountain gorilla, leatherback turtles, the Sumatran orangutans, Asian elephants, the remaining black rhinos, dammit, the bees! They are all going home, Sid – slowly passing back into the mystery. Isn't that the Rapture? Doesn't it mean it's begun? God has a covenant with all living things, you know Sid, not just with humans. Right back from the days of Noah. And now the world is dying. Like a bee laden with varroa mites, the Earth can no longer carry its human infestation. The time has come to move out of form and back into formlessness. It's time to start the journey. The animals are going into the ark."

"Jeepers." Sid looks at her, lost for words. He knows even less about the Rapture than about formlessness. Rosie was raised a Strict

63 The Simplicity Testimony is sometimes rendered as "Simplicity and Integrity Testimony".
64 Based on John 3:30: "He must increase, but I must decrease."

Baptist, though she became a spiritual gypsy years ago, and her soul is like a caddis fly larva now, resplendent in a glamorous mosaic shell decorated with wisdom memorabilia from every world religion you care to name. But if he doesn't allow himself to be distracted by externals, Sid sees there is something more primeval going on underneath. "Rosie," he asks her, "are you afraid?"

"Oh, my dearest love," she says, "I am terrified. Terrified. But whatever is to come – and I truly believe we have raped and pillaged this poor Earth beyond what is compatible with life; tar sands, fracking, these are the end-game – I mean to bear it with grace. 'When these things come to pass,' Jesus said, 'look up. Lift up your heads. Because your redemption' – whatever he meant by that – 'is drawing near'."[65]

Sid nods. "OK," he says carefully. He can feel that she is trusting him with what really matters to her. It would be so easy to belittle this, in a clumsy attempt to reassure, and he doesn't want to do that. "But – honey – if life as we know it is ending, and maybe the scientists are right and it is; what in the world difference will it make if you lose weight?"

Rosie looks lost for a moment, like a child. "I don't know," she admits. "Maybe it's one small thing I feel I can still control. And so that in the time left, I at least have a body that can run, that can dance, as well as one that has learned to live on less. And..." she pauses, frowning, thinking. "And because my body is a temple of the Holy Spirit. I want to make it all de-toxed, simple and holy, so it can be a two-way flow. As I travel out into the formless, so the formless can come and abide here in me. So long as I live, Sid, I want to be a lightning conductor, a conduit for the Light. I want to be light: travel light, live light. I just thought losing fifty-six pounds might somehow be part of that."

He reaches across the table and takes her hand. We could talk

---

65 Based on Luke 21:28: "And when these things begin to come to pass, then look up, and lift up your heads; for your redemption draweth nigh."

about loving, he thinks, about compassion and self-restraint, about walking simply and humbly with God. But maybe another day.

For sharing and wondering

- How do you personally cope with worrying world events and news items?
- What particular insights and wisdom might the Christian faith have to offer the global community facing the difficult decisions and grave challenges presented by climate change?
- What do you think it means, in practical everyday terms, to be a temple of the Holy Spirit?

Into the Mystery

Give us grace, dear Lord, to open ourselves more and more to the light and beauty of your presence. May the upwelling of your fountain of peace and love in our innermost core spill over into the disciplines and habits of our daily lives. May we walk every day, consciously, in the light of your presence.

32

Ordinary Time – Disapproval

"In the 1970s," says Rosie, sitting on the edge of the bed in her nightie, combing her hair, "my brother-in-law sang in a punk rock band. Almost everyone I knew went to punk rock concerts then. My boyfriend played bass guitar in a punk rock band, too. His band was called Pungent. My brother-in-law's was called Solid Waste. I went to one of their concerts. I remember it well. 'We're gonna sing you a little love song, called *Sick on You*.' Extraordinary."

Her hand holding the comb comes to rest in her lap, as she gazes down at the garden through the huge, low window – one of the glories of this airy room. "I sometimes used to think we could get up a punk rock band with the members of our church choir. Call it Oozing Disapproval."

Sid laughed. "That bad?" he said, sympathetically.

"Oh, yes," she answered, glancing round at him, her face serious. "Disapproval, Sid. You know what? I'm sick of it. It's stalked me all my life. It was one of the things that put me off church. Do you remember, back in 2014, the Eurovision Song Contest? A cross-dressing man with a beard won it. The Austrian entry. Over in Russia, representatives of the Orthodox Church denounced the man, the competition and the result in the roundest possible terms – 'sodomy', 'abomination', all that sort of vocabulary. Someone posted a photo of Russian Orthodox clergy in full regalia, remarking on bearded men in frocks denouncing a bearded man in a frock, and the world burst out laughing. But disapproval sits around religion like a bad smell. It's all part of the power game. Control. Struggling for supremacy. 'Jesus is *Lord*'."

"I see." Sid risks a joke. "And you disapprove of this?"

"Ha!" Rosie responds with a short, mirthless bark of bitter laughter. "Do I disapprove? Sid, I disapprove of everything. My entire life is steeped in disapproval, soaked in it. I was guided and controlled by the judicious application of shame throughout my childhood, trotting like a little dog at my mother's heels, always hoping to win her approval. As an adult – why, look at me! My step-children disapprove of me, your ex-wife disapproves of me, my ex-husband's wife disapproves of me, his family disapprove of me, all the churches I've left disapprove of me. Sid, almost everyone I've ever met disapproves of me. Even my grandson. Even the cat. I disapprove of myself. I look down at my body in the bath and I think, 'Rosie, you look like a bloated cow.' I look back at my life, at the things I've done wrong and the people I've hurt and the stupid indiscretions I've made, and I disapprove of me. I feel ashamed. Sid, I do believe if I could shed the weight of disapproval that clags and clogs my whole being, I'd tip the scales at seventy pounds. Not kilograms – pounds."

Oh dear. Sid wonders what to say. But she hasn't finished. "What about Quakers, Sid? Do they disapprove of everything, too?"

He smiles. "Well… the mainstream ones are a fairly laid-back lot. The conservative Quakers are more… er… they are silent; I mean they hold back from judgment and condemnation, but… they have a way of letting you know how they feel. And my childhood – in a Catholic family – was formed and guided by disapproval, same as yours. But that's… I mean, isn't that how society is shaped? What would you rather have? Anything goes?"

In a restless gesture of futility Rosie chucks the comb back on the bed. She stands up, resignation writ plain in her face, and picks up the clothes discarded last night. She stands holding them in her arms.

"Jesus, then?" She doesn't look at Sid, but he feels a certain weight of responsibility as she asks, "Does Jesus disapprove of everything? Does Jesus disapprove of me?"

She glances briefly at Sid. "I mean, I never do anything good or noble. I just live. I don't give people money or serve soup to the homeless or campaign for anything much. What's to approve of in my life?"

"Um…" Sid searches for a reply. "I'm not a hundred per cent sure I'm qualified to speak for Jesus. From what I've read, yes, there were some behaviours he thought very little of indeed. But he also… there's a thing in the Bible, I wrote it down somewhere once and learned it: He 'needed not that any should testify of man: for he knew what was in man.'[66] Disapproval has to do with opinions, doesn't it? Good opinion is approval. And it seems Jesus saw right past opinions to what was really there. Isn't that – well, isn't that more *understanding*?"

Rosie is looking at him now.

"You think," she says, "Jesus understands?"

Sid frowns, concentrating, digging deep. "Understands, yes; and forgives. As I see it – and I don't know if I've got it right or not – forgiveness acts like a kind of solvent for all this disapproval that clags up our insides. De-toxification. It rinses it all away, so that we can step free and walk easy. Even whatever other people may think of us or say about us. It saturates us, blocked solid as we are by a lifetime of disapproving and being disapproved of, and lets us start again."

"Well, if that's so – " Rosie's gaze is intensifying into her habitual ferocity now – "and the church is supposedly a community of the forgiven, how come it's so *rife* with disapproval?"

Sid shakes his head. "There's no point, Rosie," he says gently. "You're on a wild goose chase. How can you help anything by disapproving of people disapproving? It's no good. You just have to

66   John 2:25.

start humming a different tune. Let them approve, disapprove, who cares, leave them to it. Once you've stumbled on the fruitlessness of it, you find yourself with a new responsibility. Christ is calling you to be one of those who understand. Fear and shame is why people disapprove. Wanting to be in the right. Afraid of being rejected and made wrong. Another thing Jesus said, 'Who comes to me I will in no wise cast out.'[67] Acceptance, that is. Let other people think what they like, take the road of understanding and acceptance and that'll get you where you want to be, a place where at least you can breathe easy. A place where forgiveness has a chance to put down roots."

Hope has come into her eyes, but she looks not entirely convinced, so he ploughs on: "Something we Friends have to offer, if it's any use, is silence. I mean, of course nothing can be more loudly disapproving than silence, but at least silence is fluid. Change can happen in it. In silence, disapproval can thaw, understanding and acceptance begin. Once you've formulated an attitude in words, it's harder to retract it. Words once spoken can never be recalled. And so many of our perceptions are mistaken. How many of us really – like Jesus – know what is in people's hearts? We think we know, but we judge by what we see. There's a time to speak up – where we see cruelty, or injustice, where someone is bullied or in peril – for sure. But in the ordinary things, I for one have often been glad later when I wasn't too quick to express an opinion. Silence gives disapproval a chance to subside."

Rosie nods. She turns to go, heading for the shower.

"Rosie!" She looks back, sees the love in his eyes. "I approve of you. It's like Rumi said: 'Come even though you have broken your vows a thousand times. Come, and come yet again. Ours is not a caravan of despair.'"[68]

67 John 6:37; paraphrase of KJV.
68 These famous words of Rumi are subject to variation in different sources.

For sharing and wondering

- What part do approval and disapproval play in your life?
- Think of an experience in your own life when you felt healed by being forgiven…
- … and a time when you felt set free by being able to forgive.

Into the Mystery

Loving God, you are always eager to cleanse and heal us, to forgive us and help us start again. Give us the grace to make space in our hearts for that wonderful new beginning, not just now and again, but every single day.

33

Feast of St Benedict

"That crow," says Sid to Rosie as they sit down for their breakfast, "is the first up, without fail, every morning. Now in the summer, and in the depths of the winter as well. I can remember way back in December, opening the bathroom window even though it was cold, listening for the first bird up. Always the crow. Even while the owl is still hunting, the crow is up. Before the seagulls, before the blackbird – in the darkness, before the dawn, the first buoyant, curious 'Ark!' And when I hear it I always think of St Benedict, and what put me in mind of it is that it's St Benedict's day today."

"Why," asks Rosie, pouring their tea now it's brewed, "does that crow make you think of St Benedict?"

"They go together. Thanks," says Sid, drawing his mug of tea across the table to stand by his cereal bowl. "St Gregory the Great writes about Benedict feeding a crow in the woods, and Benedict is often depicted with – or represented by the picture of – a crow. I guess also it must be because the Benedictine habit is black. I mean, they look like crows, don't they?

"Also," he says, taking a mouthful of his cereal before it gets too soggy, "there's something about crows that's a lot like Benedictine monks. They're friendly, but kind of wary – they don't let you get too close. They always remember they're a different species, and they keep themselves to themselves, much as monastics do. You're in, or you're out – you're a crow, or you're not. That's how it is. And

159

as well as that, there's something about the Benedictines… how can I put it… something sort of polished and suave. Composed, they are. Educated. Intelligent. *Urbane*, somehow, for all their humility and simplicity. And that quiet, sly sense of humour – Rosie, *just like crows*! Whoever first saw crows as the emblem of the Benedictines knew both of them well.

"And the Benedictines are watchful, and they are up before the dawn, praying the day in. Which it would seem our own holy crow does, just the same."

"St Benedict…" Rosie muses. "Isn't he… Didn't he write the first monastic Rule? Isn't he something of a foundation in the world of monastic community?"

"In the Western church, yes. Though he did crib from the Rule of St Basil, which was about 160 years earlier, to be fair. But you're right – the Roman Catholic monastic system rests heavily on the foundation stone of the Rule of St Benedict. Have you read it?"

Rosie shakes her head. "No. Do we have a copy? Is it boring?"

Sid laughs. "Surprisingly not, and yes – we do. It's a very pious document of course, as you would expect, but what intrigues and delights me about it is how very *practical* it is. I suppose you don't have to give it much thought to realize that if you're actually going to live this – be a community, day in and day out – airy-fairy isn't going to cut it. You've got to have your head screwed on. And Benedict certainly did.

"He knew the value of silence. I love it that Benedict laid down for his monks to go into silence after Compline – the last office, as night fell. That was what they call the 'Great Silence', through the deep hours of the night right through until after Prime, the daybreak office. I always used to think the Great Silence was all spiritual, and then I noticed while my kids were growing up that the hot spots for squabbles were late in the day when they were beginning to get tired and when they'd just got up but not had breakfast yet. And I thought, oh Benedict, I *see*! Why don't we all do this?

"Someone said to me once – and this was no Benedictine but a Carmelite nun, a Sister Helena – that she thought the natural condition of a human being was silence. I had to think about that. It intrigued me, fascinated me; I wondered whether or not it was true. People think language is about communication, but I'm not sure it is. Language is necessary for the development of ideas – of abstract thinking and intellect. It doesn't just *express* thought; language grows it on as well. People who, for one reason or another, grow up without language, live in a strikingly concrete, immediate, uncomplicated world. But the best communication, the deepest communion, where ego boundaries drop and souls merge, belongs to silence. Always. That's why the terminology of the mystic refers to being in love, to sex. Only rapt in silence can you penetrate and be penetrated by the being of the Beloved."

"Like snails mating?" suggests Rosie.

"Yes," says Sid, "exactly like that."

He eats the last of his breakfast and takes a swig of tea. "There's that story in the Bible about the resurrection," he adds, "where it says that Jesus came and stood among them even though the doors were closed.[69] I've often thought of that as an icon of the silence of monastic community. The deep friendship – fellowship – that arises in their life together, below and beyond words. Mystery. Acceptance. Actual love. Nothing sentimental, mark you, and nothing effusive – a very humble, simple, practical thing."

"In my childhood," remarks Rosie, "silence was more used to shut people out. I can remember wanting to watch a comedy programme on the TV my mother disapproved of. Her silence behind the disdainfully raised newspaper was louder than words. And she didn't like my friends. Nor did my sister. When I brought someone home, it was always to a silent house. If I took them along to the kitchen to make a cup of tea, you might see a slight disturbance of the air, the vibrational wake of a person vanishing into another

69 John 20:19, 26.

room, but no other sign of inhabitation whatsoever. 'Push off' was what our silence said."

Sid grins. "I think I've heard that said – courteously, mind, and with restraint – in monastic silence, too," he says. "But Benedict didn't imagine a grim silence; not fast about you like a prison cell. He more had in mind an airy silence – something full of light and expectancy."

"Like your crow," says Rosie, "on the very tippy-top twigs of the tallest tree. As near heaven as can be."

"Something like that," agrees Sid, "but inside you."

For sharing and wondering

- What are your favourite birds?
- How do you feel about silence?
- What is your true spiritual family?

Into the Mystery

God of love, you call us to live responsibly in our world, building peace and trust loving our neighbour. Help us each to find our own vocation in the circumstances where you have set us, working quietly to bring your Kingdom into being in our homes and lives and workplaces.

34

Ordinary Time – "You have enough"

Rosie wanders into Sid's study in search of some sticky tape with which to pack up a parcel. She stoops to kiss the back of his neck, as he sits bent over the correspondence he's working through, and she continues to stand by his desk, her hand draped gently on his shoulder, just enjoying the feel of him, his presence, his vibrational field. He glances up and smiles at her, and sees her eyes resting on the calligraphy he printed off from the internet, stuck to the wall above the printer.

It's the work of the Buddhist monk Thich Nhat Hanh, and it says simply, in the great teacher's characteristic script, "You have enough".

Rosie doesn't stop looking at it, but she is aware of Sid's gaze tracking hers.

"'You have enough'," she murmurs, thoughtfully. "That makes me feel so guilty. I've been looking for some new winter boots. I've found some I like – really lovely ones – and I tell you what, they are not the cheapest. No, sir! 'You have enough.' I bet Thich Nhat Hanh only has cheap sandals and bare feet. Or socks hand-knitted by nuns. I bet in the winter he only has cheap trainers. Not really nice leather boots. 'You have enough.' Maybe I do. How would I know?"

Sid reaches his arm round her waist and hugs her to him, laughing.

"You can have your lovely winter boots," he says. "I'll buy them for you, as a present. How much are they?"

She hesitates. "I'm not sure I should tell you," she says eventually. "I meant it when I said they aren't the cheapest. I mean, I have got the money, but… 'You have enough'."

"Well," says Sid, "the thing is, that can mean more than you're thinking. That's the joy of it. In the world of Mammon, everything is about money and counting the cost. Everything mean and scarce and penny-pinching. In the sacred economy, it isn't like that. It doesn't matter if you're rich or poor, if you're absolutely loaded or you haven't a bean.

"It's all about currency. People – perseveringly coached by Mammon – mistakenly believe 'currency' means 'money'; but it doesn't, it means 'flow'. So, you don't need to grab it or clutch it, that's a waste of time. If you sit by a river, watching the flow, and you want to drink some – don't, by the way; river water has parasites and whatnot, this is just an example – it's no good reaching in and trying to grab a tight fistful. It all squidges out and you end up with none. You have to open your hand in the stream and let it flow in, bring it out brimful and dripping again and again.

"That's how it works with the sacred economy. It's all gift, all flow, you just open your hand in the stream. One way of looking at it you have nothing, the other way, you have everything. It's all currency, just a flowing. So when you look at this thing that says 'You have enough', it could mean, 'You can rest in contentment and peace, you don't need to be always striving and grabbing and snatching.' Or, it could mean, 'It'll be OK; you don't need to worry. God has it covered. He knows you need some winter boots. There'll be enough for you to have a pair of boots, Rosie.'"

Sid gives her a squeeze. "You worry too much, my darling. We have enough. Let me buy you the boots."

Rosie nods, thoughtfully. "Thank you," she answers him, simply. "It's just… there have been times when I've been so poor. When I didn't know where the money would come from. There was nothing left."

"And – did you pay your bills?" asks Sid. "Where *did* the money come from?"

"Oh, I did – always," she says, emphatically. "I used to pray and pray. And sometimes there'd be an envelope on the mat that someone had slipped through the door. Sometimes a friend round for coffee would tuck a little roll of notes in my hand as they were leaving. Sometimes I'd get some work in, just in the nick of time. I don't know how we got through, but we did."

"And maybe," says Sid, "sometimes you were the friend who pushed the money through the door, who stopped to drop a handful of coins into the hat of a busker, who paid to get a homeless dog a place in a shelter?"

"Yes. Of course," she says.

"That's the currency," Sid says, "that's the flow. That's the sacred economy. What Jesus said – 'give, and it will be given to you. A good measure, pressed down, shaken together, running over, will be put into your lap; for the measure you give will be the measure you get back.'[70] But before you begin to panic – because I know what you're like, Rosie my love – that's about generosity, not about tit-for-tat. He's the one who starts the ball rolling, the first to give. This is God we're talking about – it can't *run out*. He's just saying, don't be nervous, there's no need to hold back; don't hoard stuff and lock it away. Just share it and give it and have fun with it. You have enough."

Rosie nods. "I always did have enough, too," she says. "In the whole of my life, my budget never worked on paper, but somehow we always paid our bills and always had something for a loaf of bread and a tin of beans. And I knew where the wild blackberries grew and the good places to pick up dropped fruit and vegetables when the market closed down in the evening. And I never lived anywhere that had no open fire or woodstove, just in case we ran

70 Luke 6:38 NRSV.

out of money for the electricity. I thought we could keep warm by making fires of all the junk mail.

"And I remember thinking, those days were the time of miracles. Because, how can you see a miracle of provision unless there is some lack, something you need? There's no wonder rich nations slide into atheism and humanism. It is the poor who can testify to the providence of God. Even so, it does leave its scars – a habit of anxiety.

"Oh, Sid, I remember one afternoon in the school summer holidays, when we had so little in hand. I'd scraped enough together to buy a loaf of bread and a carton of milk, and we had tea bags and a can of beans in the cupboard. We took the children to a fair – free entry advertised. But when we got there, though there was no admission charge, there were men either side of the gate rattling buckets for *donations*. And I just lost it. Screamed at them that I hardly had money for bread; that we'd come because they *said it was free*. I felt so embarrassed, so ashamed."

"Ah, my Rosie." Sid rests his head against her, holding her close; comforting. "The thing is, sweetheart… even then – you had enough. The problem was the shame and embarrassment, the anxiety. Those are the things to let go of, if you can. In the stream of grace, you open your hand and just let them go. It's for washing away all the bad stuff, as well as for providing what you need. Those words – 'You have enough' – that's really a prayer. I mean, it's God that has enough – that's the reason *we* do."

For sharing and wondering

- If you could wave a magic wand to change one particular circumstance for the better, which one would you choose to change?

- Can you think of an occasion in your life when someone's kindness to you made all the difference?

- What are the initiatives in the neighbourhood where you live, to help people who are poor and in need? In what ways might you be able to contribute to their work?

Into the Mystery

Generous God, you invite us to share in your work of healing and grace, by letting your kindness flow through us. Help us to love unconditionally, to welcome wholeheartedly, to give without a second thought. Help us to be numbered among those making the world a warmer and more cheerful place: count us among the helpers.

35

Ordinary Time – Letting Your Life Speak

"Honey, can you spare a moment? I need a pair of hands to hold this picture up, so I hang it right."

"Be right there. Just a sec – I'm almost done."

Rosie does not – would not – confess that what she is in the middle of is a game of online Solitaire. She hopes it sounds as though she's involved in a bank transaction or dealing with important correspondence. Nothing in Rosie's upbringing makes it OK to require someone to wait until you finish a game. Guiltily she closes the page down as soon as she sees this round won't work out.

Not that Sid is ever critical of her spending time playing. The critics are all in her head, the voices of parents and teachers internalized years ago. Sid believes in games. As she stands beside him now, holding the painting in place against the wall, she recalls a conversation from the previous weekend, when she expressed frustration at herself for wanting to stop and play.

"Playing Solitaire is a total waste of time," she said to Sid then.

"D'you think so?" he countered. "I can think of some very valuable aspects to it."

"Such as?"

"Well, you have to keep your wits about you, to notice potential connections. And you have to be very patient – they used to call it

168

'Patience' in the old days of actual playing cards, didn't they? If it doesn't work out – and it often doesn't – you have to just accept it and start again. That's an excellent life lesson!"

According to Sid, your whole life can be an acted prophecy, or acted intercession. He likes to recall the words of George Fox, founder of the Society of Friends and possibly Sid's No. 1 hero: "Let your life preach."

As the years have gone by and the Society has grown uneasy with its Christian roots, there have been little attempts to kick dust over those uncompromising origins. "Let your life speak," they represent their founder as having said, these days. But Sid knows. It wasn't that. George Fox said, "Let your life *preach*." After all, "speak", what's that? Everyone's life speaks. Some people's just prattle on inanely, others are like a torrent of abuse, some are a critical commentary, some an unending song of complaint. Some lives trail about announcing sadly, "Nobody wants to see my old face..." A self-fulfilling prophecy. But Fox meant by demeanour and action, by choice and attitude, by habit and occupation, to steadily proclaim the gospel.

Sid's other two heroes, shoulder to shoulder with George Fox, John Woolman, Isaac Penington and William Penn on the living room mantelpiece of Sid's soul's interior home, are Mohandas Gandhi and Francesco Bernadone – the latter became St Francis of Assisi.

They too placed solid emphasis on the silent proclamation of lived faith. St Francis said, "It's no use walking anywhere to preach unless our preaching is in our walking," to which Sid's heart adds its own robust "Amen!"

Gandhi told his followers to "Be the change that you wish to see in the world." One time when he was on a train just pulling out of the station, a reporter came puffing up hoping to secure a quote for his paper from the great man. "Have you any message for us?" he panted. Gandhi scribbled on a scrap of paper, "My life is my message"; words that have been enshrined in history.

It's a personal thing, Sid thinks, the message of one's life. Unique. A life's own song. An individual's own particular take on things. But it can also preach, and prophesy, and pray; for a life calls out to God and proclaims a belief system in every living minute. A life is never hypocritical, it is simply truthful. Where words and deeds don't match up, what does that mean? Sometimes that the person is afraid of exclusion or getting things wrong or being in trouble. Sometimes that they stand to gain from acquiescing to someone else's dogma – money or work or status, usually. Sometimes they are merely parroting ideas inculcated long since, never really believing them but vaguely revering them as the remote gods of tradition. But a life tells the truth, all right – including the measurable gap between what it says and what it does. So Sid thinks, anyway.

Right now, he knocks the nail in – it's not a heavy picture, it doesn't need a rawl plug and a screw, a little wire nail will do the trick.

"Thanks, sweetie," he says cheerfully. "As you were. What were you up to? Playing Solitaire?"

Rosie freezes. Pauses. "Yes," she admits reluctantly, in a small voice.

"Goodo," says Sid, with a smile. "Shall we have a game of Scrabble, later on?"

She watches him strolling down the garden, taking the hammer and nails back to their place in the toolshed, stopping on the way to bend and stroke their tabby cat, who winds round Sid's legs, butting a furry head against his calves in trust and affection.

She thinks about his opinion that everyone's life is an acted prophecy, an acted prayer. Sid's life, she decides, is praying quietly; words of humility and gratitude. Sid's life says, "There but for the grace of God go I," and likes to give other people the benefit of the doubt, help them out where he can.

And its acted prophecy? Its message to the world? Something hopeful, and simple, she thinks. Something about small acts of kindness adding up to make life worth living. About ordinary human loving, in all its vulnerability. Having the forbearance to go on choosing cheerfulness, and the courage to trust – to offer the truth of oneself and let it be enough.

These things, she decides, I read in his life. More like jottings on the back of an envelope than a five-page, twenty-minute sermon.

She goes back to the computer and opens the page again, "Free On-line Solitaire". Rosie makes a decision. From now on, she will not feel guilty for playing – for relaxing, and having fun, and taking time out. If there is a choice – and why not? – from this moment on, she will let the acted prophecy of her life announce to anyone who cares to pay attention: it is OK to play. To dawdle and hum, to add bubbles to the bathwater, to watch daytime TV and meet a friend in town for a coffee.

Did you hear that, world? It is OK to play!

For sharing and wondering

- Think of three people you know – one of your parents, a famous celebrity, a neighbour. So far as you can encapsulate it in words, what do you perceive to be the message of the life of each of those people?

- Imagine you have given yourself permission for a play day, doing just what makes you happy. How would you spend that day?

- When you were a child growing up, what was the attitude to leisure and play in your family?

Into the Mystery

Joyous God, fountain of all life, we think of you delighting in creation, exclaiming over all you have made, "Oh, that's good!" We imagine you as an artist, dreaming up the amazing shapes and colours of flowers, birds, animals, deep-sea fish, sunsets and northern lights. Your playing and dreaming has brought to birth all the beauty we know. May we follow your example, and delight in our playing and dreaming with all its possibility and joy.

36

Ordinary Time – Taking it Literally

"The problem is," says Rosie as she heaps the salad leaves onto her plate and reaches for the bunch of tomatoes on their vine, "that people don't think the Bible is true. They don't take it literally."

Sid groaned. "Oh, God," he says, "Rosie, please don't say that. Don't even think it."

"What? Why?" She passes him the bowl of salad.

"People who take the Bible literally are a confounded nuisance. Witch-hunting, punitive inquisitorial types creating exclusion zones. Homophobic misogynistic child-beaters. Sadism looking for a peg to hang itself on, mostly. Repressed individuals starved of love and freedom, out for revenge."

"Have some of that salad will you, and then I can see what's left – I might want some more. This dressing is good, by the way. I made it just this morning. It's come out well. What you just said is not taking the Bible literally. Granted, the Bible is full of murder and violence and God telling people to start wars and stuff, and slaughter other people wholesale. But it's really a library tracking a journey out of revenge and rulebooks into compassion and the creation of peace. The folks you're talking about take little verses here and there and bend them to their own predetermined purposes. That isn't taking the Bible to be true, it's a sacrilegious appropriation of it to further corrupt personal agendas. That's not what I meant at all."

"OK," says Sid, tearing off a piece of the crusty baguette and adding a generous helping of butter to the edge of his plate. "So, what did you mean?"

"Well – excuse me talking with my mouth full – I was thinking about our bodies being temples of the Holy Spirit.[71] St Paul says, don't you realize that your bodies are temples of the Holy Spirit, who was given to you by God and lives in you. The only difficulty I have with that is, what does he mean by 'you'? Obviously 'you' is not your body – otherwise the word 'your' wouldn't apply. If it's 'your body', then the body and the 'you' are not one and the same. But the Holy Spirit and the 'you' are not one and the same either – the Holy Spirit has been given to 'you' and lives in 'you'. So there are three things there – the Holy Spirit, the 'you' and the body.

"In the story about the creation of Adam in Genesis, God makes a man out of the dust of the Earth, then breathes into the clay form he has made, and it becomes a *nephesh* – a living, spiritual being; alive. So the 'you' is not only the Earth body; it's already made up of Holy Spirit – the breath of God – but St Paul means something beyond that; the Holy Spirit as a residing gift.

"There's consciousness, then; the breath of God. And there's the gift of the Holy Spirit; inspiration, should we say? Or isn't that just the same as 'the breath of God'? I mean, 'to inspire' means 'to breathe into', doesn't it? Whatever. A double dose. But the bit I've been thinking about is about the body. Now I wasn't too sure what St Paul meant, so I looked up about it. He's using the plural 'you' – as in, all of you. So I wondered if he might mean that the body of believers, the body that you all make up, is the temple of the Holy Spirit. Not so. Apparently he means 'the body of each one of you' – so he means our Earth bodies; your body, my body. That's the temple.

"And I thought about our bodies, and how having a body... well... a body is holographic – a hologram of the universe, teeming

71   1 Corinthians 6:19.

with life. It's like a world, a planet. For one thing, it has several minds. The gut has its own intelligence, as does the immune system and the central nervous system. And emotional intelligence is different from gut instinct or intellectual process, and compassion is not any of them. As well as minds, it has populations. Hosts of bacteria, localized flocks of microscopic creatures and tiny mites. Yeast populations farmed by the bacteria. And, let's not forget, the truth is most of us are host to parasites, even if we don't know it. Not just fleas and headlice and passing things like mosquitoes, but living in the gut. So this temple we're in charge of – what are we, priests, maybe? Or vergers? Sacristans? – is absolutely heaving with... er... populations, of sorts. And then, what about our memories and all the people in there? People we knew and no longer see but still carry with us. Babies who inhabited our wombs – they affect their mother's cellular structure forever. And your sexual partners leave some of their DNA with you forever, too. Gosh, Sid, what a temple! It's like a big cathedral on a high feast day! A carnival!

"So we have this busy, thronged adobe structure where many lives are gathered, all to the glory of the resident God, the Holy Spirit, and it's our job – the job of the 'you' each one of us is – to take care of it and keep it in good shape and make sure it's fit for purpose. That's why it matters what we eat. Have some more salad."

Sid looks at the salad but thinks he's probably eaten enough leaves for the moment. He pours himself a glass of wine, and looks with satisfaction at its intense, deep, incarnadine ruby red in the cut crystal.

"But, you know, if we take that literally – if we believe it's true that our bodies are holy, a sacred space ringing with worship, with all the weird beings inside it gathered under the wing of Holy Spirit for the glory and adoration of God – well, surely it will make a difference to how we treat it and what we think is good enough for it. When we get dressed in the morning, it will be like adorning the altar – our clothes will be *vestments*. We will want to wear something *beautiful*.

And dignified. Noble. Not jazzy or frivolous or cutesy, but dignified and full of grace. And maybe we will wear jewels or garlands or something – kind of like stained glass and candles and big stands of flowers but suitable for a body. Pearls. Crystals. Precious metals and precious stones. If we can afford it, obviously. But adornments made with artistry of something real, anyway. And colours! Lovely colours. And singing. A temple should be full of music. And what we eat will be like temple offerings – beautifully presented and of the best quality we can manage. Especially because the food we eat actually becomes the material substance of the temple. We are building the temple when we eat. What do we want our temple to be made of? Monosodium glutamate and white sugar? Vodka and factory-farmed chicken? How would that bring glory to God?"

Sid nods. He's not quite sure he has anything to contribute to this. It all sounds quite exotic and busy. Like a Hindu temple or a Sikh gurdwara in full swing. Or a Catholic street procession for the feast of Corpus Christi, with banners and statues and a robed choir. He wonders if a Quaker body can be more like a meeting house – a place of silence and peace. But he doesn't want to rain on her parade, so he says nothing.

"That's what I meant," she explains, "about taking the Bible literally."

"Blimey," says Sid. "It certainly sounds exciting."

For sharing and wondering

- How would you describe the place and importance of the Bible in your own life?

- How does the way you personally care for your own body reflect your understanding of God?

- How do you understand the concept that God's Holy Spirit dwells in you?

Into the Mystery

Come, Holy Spirit, in all your radiance, all your joy. Come into the innermost chamber of our being. Enlighten our minds, fill our hearts with hope and joy, free and heal our bodies from limiting patterns and habits. Renew us and transform us according to the pattern of infinite life.

37

Lammas

"When we do Quaker grace, Sid," Rosie asks him as she picks up her fork, "what are you thinking in your head?"

This is an indication of two waymarks passed. When they first got married, Sid was too shy to ask that they share grace before they begin a meal. He did it, privately, in the Quaker silence of his own heart, but felt awkward to suggest they both overtly participate in the ritual. Eventually he felt able to say it mattered to him, and ever since then they have observed its small reverence – a silent holding of one another's hands, closed eyes, bowed head, before starting in on their food. Being able to ask about what felt like such a personal thing formed a landmark in their relationship; like one of the altars Abraham built in his desert journey into the unknown – here, too, God could be found.

The second waymark passed is apparent in Rosie being free to ask Sid the question. Perhaps used to criticism, for a long time when she made such an enquiry he would stiffen and become defensive. What was she getting at? What did she have against Quaker grace? Was she mocking it? Did she think it weird? "Getting at" used to be a recurring phrase in Sid's vocabulary. "What are you getting at?" Quite often he thought the other person was probably getting at him. But these days he has relaxed. After episodes too numerous to recount of Rosie staring at him pink-cheeked, in open-mouthed indignation, as yet another conversation degenerated into a row, he has managed to grasp that she was not getting at anything – least of all him. She was only asking a question.

And so it feels easy between them as he considers her words, and says: "Well, mostly I'm saying thank you. I'm grateful for the food, for our home, for the money to get proper nourishing stuff to eat, for a whole set-up that means we have a freezer and a stove, water all laid on. I mean, it's marvellous, isn't it, when you think about it? All this! And I'm grateful for someone to sit and eat with – share my whole life with. That's food of a kind.

"So first of all, every time, I want to say thank you. But there's also the business of blessing. In the silence I bless the food, bless our water, bless the pastures and the cornfields, the orchards and the ocean.

"I bear in mind that at the Eucharist Jesus consecrated the bread and wine by giving thanks. That's all he had to do to make it holy – take it in his hands and give thanks. It actually changed it. That's like the work of… er… what's his name? The man who did all those experiments on water. You know. The man who stuck labels on the jars of water and discovered the molecular structure of the water actually changed, depending on what he'd written on the label."

"Masaru Emoto?"

"That's the one. He started with 'Thank You'. He found that regardless of the language used, if you wrapped a label saying 'Thank You' round the jar, facing in towards the water, its atomic structure formed up into the most beautiful crystals.

"That's kind of the same thing as the Eucharist, isn't it? So that's what I'm thinking is happening when we pause for a Quaker grace. Our silent 'Thank You' – to the fields, the food, each other and all the rest of it – will bring out the potential of its beauty."

"That's nice," she comments, as Sid turns his attention to his mushroom omelette. "That sounds about the same as what goes through my head, too."

"What's more – " says Sid – "Gosh, this is tasty! Perfect. I'll cook supper tonight, if you like."

"Good – yes please. Can it be early, though, because I don't like eating after six?"

Rosie believes a body needs to rest from digestion through the long hours of the night. She really aspires to the Buddhist monastic system of eating nothing after the midday meal. But then she always gets peckish around tea-time. "But you said, 'What's more'," she prompts him.

"Did I? Oh… yes, I know. It's Lughnasadh today."

"Come again?" Rosie looks at him blankly. "Loo-what? Lasagna? That's what you're cooking tonight?"

He laughs. "No, no – that is, I can if that's what you'd fancy but it isn't what I said. Lughnasadh. The old Celtic festival. Lammas, it became – as in, Loaf-Mass. The first of the two harvest festivals – the sacrifice of John Barleycorn to feed the hungry people."

"Oh, right. When's the second one?"

"Mabon – the harvest home – that the Irish call Alban Elfed. That's the autumn equinox. This is the cross-quarter day, coming between the summer solstice and the equinox. The grain harvest started with Lammas, and all would be gathered in by Mabon.

"*Lughnasadh* is Old Gaelic. It derives from the old god Lugh. In the mythology, he held a funeral feast for his mother Tailtiu." He grins. "She died of exhaustion after clearing all the fields in Ireland in readiness to sow the crops. So it's a story about the agricultural cycle – honouring and taking seriously the death of what feeds us, plants and animals both. The giving of life to nourish us. There you are – the Eucharist again."

Rosie smiles at him. "You have a lot to say about the Eucharist for a Quaker!"

"Well… you don't ever really disconnect from your roots, do you? I grew up a Catholic. And besides… I mean, you know this, don't you? It isn't that Quakers don't have the Eucharist. They just have it all the time, everywhere. In the beginning – with George

Fox and his friends – what they wanted, was to let loose the holy. Not have it all controlled by clergy and enacted in steeple-houses, as they called them. They didn't want to trash or forget the Eucharist. They wanted to say, every meal is a Eucharist, even in the humblest cottage. Every encounter is sacred. It's nothing to do with special buildings or dogma or priesthoods. You can't package the holy and dole it out and control who gets a share. It's free. It's wild.

"So you and me sitting down for our omelette at Lammas, holding hands and keeping holy silence, giving thanks in our hearts as a blessing on our food – that's Eucharist."

Rosie smiles at him. "With you, it ain't just Low Mass, either," she says. "It's the whole works – we get a sermon and everything!"

He goes suddenly still, looks embarrassed.

"Oh for heaven's sake, Sid! I'm only teasing you! I love it. I love you. Do you think I would have married a man who doesn't know how to think?"

But the enthusiasm is doused. She sighs. "I'll put the kettle on. Cup of tea, sweetheart? Oh, come on! I have cookies…"

He smiles again; and this is his gift to her. This too is Eucharist. This love.

For sharing and wondering

- Do you have – or would you like to have – a tradition of grace before meals? What form does it (or could it) take?

- What recent encounters in daily life can you think of that speak to you of Eucharist?

- What would you especially like to give thanks for in your life at the present time?

Into the Mystery

God of abundant provision, we thank you for your kindness, for all the goodness and love that has flowed into our lives. Help us to trust you in every circumstance, to walk close to you through every twist and turn of our lives. Help us to see in every landscape through which our journey onward leads, something of beauty, something of hope, something that speaks to us of grace and goodness.

38

Ordinary Time – The Name of Jesus

"What d'you make of this, Sid?"

He wanted to finish the novel he's reading, really. Only four pages to go. But Sid has a rule of life, and he lives by it: people before things. So he lifts his head and does his best to sound genuinely interested. "What?"

"There are these things in the Bible," says Rosie. "I've collected them and written them down. Listen. 'The name of the Lord is a strong tower: the righteous runneth into it, and is safe.'[72] Then this: 'For whosoever shall call upon the name of the Lord shall be saved.'[73] And this: 'And it shall come to pass, that whosoever shall call upon the name of the Lord shall be saved.'[74] And finally, this: 'Believe in the Lord Jesus, and you will be saved – you and your household.'[75] What do you make of that?"

Sid frowns, puzzled. This doesn't sound complicated, or hard to understand. "Er... well... I guess if you put it all together it just means that if you believe in the name of the Lord Jesus, and call on his name and take refuge in it, you will be saved. Doesn't it?"

"Saved from what?"

72 Proverbs 18:10.
73 Romans 10:13.
74 Acts 2:21.
75 Acts 16:31 NIV.

"Sin? Hell? Being lost? Damnation?"

"It means you'll go to heaven, you think?"

"Oh – a bit more than that. I think it means your life will start to transform from the very middle. It will begin to grow peace and joy at the core. Cynicism and meanness will shed off you. New habits of hope and trust will start to form. It's that other thing – 'if anyone is in Christ, he is a new creation; old things have passed away; behold, all things have become new.'[76] Because the name of the Lord Jesus is the living Word of God. 'For the word of God is alive and active. Sharper than any double-edged sword, it penetrates even to dividing soul and spirit, joints and marrow; it judges the thoughts and attitudes of the heart.'[77] If you have something alive and active in the middle of you, that you've invited into your soul – or equally if you've invoked it, taken refuge in it – then it'll change you. Bound to. 'Be not conformed to this world: but be ye transformed by the renewing of your mind.'"[78]

"Gosh." Rosie looks at him, impressed. "How do you just know all those things? How come you can remember them without writing them down?"

Sid smiles. "They just stick in my mind. I've thought about them, I suppose. Turned them over and over and wondered about them."

"What do you think it means, Sid, to believe in the name of Jesus – to take refuge in the name of the Lord? And, what if you *don't* believe? Surely you can only believe what you think is true. And surely you won't think all the stuff about Jesus is true if, say, the parish priest abused you sexually when you were a seven-year-old choirboy, or your very religious father and mother beat you senseless and screamed hateful insults in your face? Why would Jesus hold that against you? It's got to be real, hasn't it? You know, the Inquisition and so on – where people had to recant their heresies and acquiesce to whatever doctrine was the flavour of the month or be burned at

76 2 Corinthians 5:17 NKJV.
77 Hebrews 4:12 NIV.
78 Romans 12:2.

the stake – as well as barbaric, that has to be the epitome of stupid. You can't *make* people believe, and you can't make yourself believe. You either believe or you don't. End of."

Sid grimaces his doubt. "Hmm… no… I don't think that's what it means really."

"Well, that's why I was asking you," says Rosie. "I don't think that's what it means either. So what does it mean?"

"OK." Sid resigns himself to this and closes his book, puts it down. "The Name of Jesus is not a word. That's the first mistake people make – in trying to reduce this whole process to words. It all goes back to when God revealed himself to Moses in the Old Testament, and told him that the name of God is 'I Am That I Am'.[79] So the name of the Lord on which we can call is not an epithet or a label – it's the actual being of God, his essential self. What came to be called the *ego eimi*. This has not very much to do with creeds and a whole big lot to do with how you behave, the choices you make, the person you become, the way you shape your life. What Jesus said – 'By their fruits ye shall know them.'[80]

"I think people get muddled up. They confuse the *name* of God and Jesus being the *Word* of God with a notion that salvation boils down to *saying the right words* – pray this and you'll get a ticket to heaven. But it isn't like that.

"In the old Hebrew language, the breath of God – *ruach* – is the same as the Spirit of God. It's all striving to express that everything about God is primary, first principle – 'Ground of our Being' as good old Tillich put it.[81] God cannot be put into words. Someone's breath is their very life – so Jesus is the out-breathed spiritual expression of who God actually is.

"What it all amounts to is that if who you really are seeks the heart of… finds communion with… takes refuge in… cries out to

79 Exodus 3:14.
80 Matthew 7:20.
81 Paul Tillich, German American systemic theologian, writer of *The Courage To Be* (1952), *Dynamics of Faith* (1957), and *Systemic Theology* (in 3 vols, 1951–63).

and yearns for... goodness me, this is so hard to say... Start again. If the heart of you is conjoined with the heart of God, then healing is inevitable."

"What about this that says 'you and all your household', then? Surely you can't make choices for somebody else."

"Yes and no," says Sid. "You must have noticed that if one person in a group changes, the whole dynamic shifts? Influence, catching force. It's exactly because this is about real transformation, not just signing up to a formulaic doctrine. It doesn't mean that if you acquiesce to the creeds you get a group get-out-of-hell-free card. It means that if you're plugged into God you become luminous; you show everyone around you the way. You don't intend or expect it – it just happens. Look, Rosie – I'm so sorry – would you mind if I just finish off reading this book?"

"Oh – no, that's OK. I was going to start making the soup in any case. I just wanted to get that straight."

For sharing and wondering

- Would you describe yourself as "saved"? What do you think that expression really means?

- Can you think of a time when a friendship with a particular person, or belonging to a group, influenced you and made a change in your life?

- When you are troubled and afraid, in what do you seek comfort or take refuge?

Into the Mystery

In so many and varied ways you hold out lifelines of hope to us, O God. Through the beauty and poetry of great art, music and literature, through the companionship of our personal relationships, through the inspiration of noble souls, through the teaching of the Bible, through prayer and worship – even through the comfort of food and drink, the warmth and peace of our homes. Thank you for our shelters from life's storms, thank you for the goodness of your love. May we never forget by whose hand they were given; may we always, in the end, find our refuge in you.

39

Feast of St Clare of Assisi

"Maya Angelou," says Rosie, watching Sid prep the veggies for the curry, "wrote a poem about a caged bird singing and a book about it, didn't she?"

"She did," says Sid, halving the onion, turning the cut sides down onto the chopping board and making the incisions towards the root that he will cut across to create the diced pieces. "And her book took its title from another poem about a caged bird by Paul Dunbar. It's an archetype in its way, don't you think – the caged bird? If you think of William Blake writing that 'A robin redbreast in a cage puts all heaven in a rage', or Gerard Manley Hopkins' poem about the 'dare-gale skylark scanted in a dull cage'. Always reminds me of St Clare of Assisi."

"Really? Did she write poetry? Shall I peel the garlic for you while you cut up those courgettes?"

"Ah! My angel! Thank you very much – here. Well, she did write poetry, but that isn't what I meant. I was thinking more of the caged bird. Clare was the child of a nobleman – his eldest daughter – hemmed about with expectations from the start. She had such spirit, such fire. A marriage was fixed up for her when she was just a young teenager, but she dodged that one, asking to have it put off until she was eighteen. And then – oh, thanks, honey." He takes the peeled garlic from her, chops it fine, adds it to the cut onions and courgettes, and begins to dice the tomatoes. "Then she heard St Francis preach, and that was it for Clare – she knew what she wanted."

Rosie has fetched the box of spices for him from the cupboard, and Sid turns on the flame under the heavy pan with its coconut oil, adding the mustard seeds first, holding them over the heat until they begin to pop.

"Clare crept out of the family mansion by a little back door – the door of the dead, where bodies of the deceased were removed – during the night, and went to find Francis, asking to be accepted into the wave of simplicity and absolute devotion he had pioneered. And he accepted her. He – personally – cut off her long hair as a sign of her renunciation of the world. Her death to the world. All on something of a euphoric cloud of fervour, I think; because then they had to deal with the question, now what?"

The spices mustn't fry too long or they burn. Sid turns down the heat and adds the onions and garlic, moving them around, watching over them.

"I don't know what St Clare imagined would be happening, but I have a strong suspicion she thought she'd be mucking in with the men – she was the first woman to follow in the feet of St Francis. I think she saw herself helping the poor, living in a makeshift hut, washing the feet of lepers, serving the dispossessed, lifting people out of despair."

Once the tomatoes are in, Sid adds lentils and some water. Then bouillon mix. He puts the lid on the pan and turns back to the table where Rosie has cleared away the garlic and onion peel. "Tea, Sid?" she asks, filling the kettle.

"You bet!" Sid wipes down the table, washes his hands, and sits down while she makes their mugs of tea.

"I think she just answered the call of Christ in her heart," he says. "I don't believe for a moment she projected forward, thought it through. And instead of a life of freedom with the friars, what happened? Francis found a place for her in a Benedictine house with some enclosed nuns, and that's the way it was from then on. She did get nearer to him. San Damiano – the church he rebuilt with his own hands – became the centre of the order she founded. She wanted the same life of radical poverty as Francis had, and this met with stiff opposition; it was unthinkable for women – too hard, too austere. But she was the first woman in history to write her own rule of life – go, St Clare! Thanks, honey."

Sid takes the mug of steaming tea and (after a brief unsuccessful struggle of willpower) the cookie she offers him too.

"She had to fight the authorities all her life to get her vision of absolute simplicity enshrined in her rule. She kept in touch with Francis too – they were good friends. He sought, and got, wise counsel from Clare.

"But that life of enclosure, I've often wondered. Was that the real renunciation, for her? A dare-gale skylark scanted in a dull cage. Poor Clares, well, there's nobody like them. They have such a forthright, sturdy spirit. A practical, cheerful piety. Such a can-do approach to life. And Clare… she was inspired. They said when she came from prayer, her face shone enough to dazzle them."

"So," says Rosie, "if Clare had been born in, say, the 1960s, you think she would never have lived that way at all?"

Sid pauses, considering. "That's right," he says then. "I think she'd have started something more like the Street Pastors or the Salvation Army. Something open and radical, bold and free. But…"

"Yes?" Rosie prompts him.

"Well, it's an odd business isn't it? Are the lives of any of us only about ourselves? I mean, whatever Clare did or didn't imagine or want for herself, she made the best of what was handed to her, without complaint. She accepted the enclosure, though she repudiated all luxuries or dilution of the Franciscan ideal. It's like the enclosure was as far as she would go and no further. As if she accepted to live the Franciscan way behind walls, but it did have to be the whole nine yards – she wouldn't compromise on the inner reality of the vision. And that was at the beginning of the thirteenth century. Francis ran her community up until 1216, but he handed over the reins to Clare then, and she held the fort until she died in 1253, in her fifties, only a few days after she finally got her rule accepted by the Pope. And Rosie – just think of all the women from then until the present day who have been called into the life of a Poor Clare. It's a beautiful order. It's a way of grace, still challenging the world, still upholding a counter-culture ideal of simplicity in a cynical age suffocating in its own complexities and consumerism. Those 'little poor ladies' have all to teach us, still.

"So what I wonder is, even though it must have felt like the hugest disappointment, the most dismal compromise of all time, to discover that while the brothers were out on the road preaching the gospel and sleeping under the stars like hobos, she was to be saying her prayers and scrubbing the floors behind bars – was it the unexpected Way? I mean the straight and narrow way that is as tough as all-get-out to come to terms with, but leads you home in the end? You and all the ones who come behind you. I don't know. I've thought about it often. And I always felt sorry for St Clare. I think she had her dream shattered, but she took the shards of it and made a new one. Like Jesus said, 'Gather up the broken bits so that nothing will be lost.'[82] It must have taken some doing, don't you think?"

Rosie nods. "It's the work of a lifetime," she says with conviction, "to craft something durable and beautiful of the bits of a broken dream that some man left you with. They should have made her the patron of new beginnings."

For sharing and wondering

- Describe one of your favourite meals.
- In what ways do you think a life dedicated to prayer can make a difference to society?
- Can you think of three people whose life and teaching have really inspired you?

82 John 6:12, my paraphrase.

Into the Mystery

In the secret chamber of our hearts, call us and speak to us, Lord Jesus. Speak to us of our vocation, draw us on to become what you have in mind for us, refine us until laziness and self-interest fall away, until we find the freedom and wisdom to be shaped according to the pattern of your love for us.

40

Ordinary Time – The Presence of Jesus

"Sid," Rosie asks him, as he stands stirring the sauce for their pasta, "would you say you know Jesus?"

"Er… yes – sure," he says somewhat absently, reaching for the *herbes de Provence*.

"What I mean is, would you say you know Jesus *personally*?"

He is paying attention now, puts the cap back on the pot of dried herbs slowly, thinking.

"Yes. Yes I would. Why?"

"Well, on Facebook last week I came across a bunch of people – keen Christians – talking about knowing Jesus personally. They were – almost – all of one mind, that this is a contemptible phrase. They saw it in terms of all-about-me exclusivism. Jesus-and-me cosy introversion that isn't what real Christianity is all about. It surprised me. They said that the phrase originated in the 1970s, which I can believe, and that before then Christianity had been a community thing and that's what it's meant to be."

"OK," says Sid, tasting his sauce and going to the shelves for the bouillon mix. "Sounds fair enough."

"Does it? You see, the thing is, I'm not really – well, you know this – a community person. I like to be by myself. If someone was strapped for cash I'd give them money; if I saw them leaning against the wall on a dark, rainy night, weeping, I'd stop to find out what was wrong; if a child was lost and frightened I'd help him find his mother; if someone was dying I'd sit with them and help them to find peace and not be afraid. But, if it's a potluck supper or a bazaar or even an extra-enthusiastic sharing of the peace, I'm out of there. And plus, I don't believe a lot of what they teach in church, and I don't find the church especially attractive, in its historical or present forms. *Christianity* is not what I love. But I do love Jesus."

The water on the back hotplate is coming up to the boil, and Sid tips in the pasta he's measured out.

"Yeah, but they go together, don't they? Isn't that the exact thing Jesus said? 'By this shall all men know that ye are my disciples. If ye have love one to another.'[83] And somewhere else I think it says: 'if we don't love people we can see, how can we love God, whom we cannot see?'[84] It's a dodgy thing to believe you love Jesus and nobody else."

Rosie is silent for a moment. Then, "I know," she says, "but I can't help that. It's how I am. It's not that I don't care about people, I just don't like parties or organizations or group experiences. There must be a place for introverts in the Kingdom of Heaven. God made me that way. Anyway, that doesn't really bother me so much. I've come to peace with who I am and what I feel about the church. I don't feel worried or guilty about that any more, it's just the way it is. I try to be kind and that's the best they get out of me. But what I found disturbing about those Christians talking on Facebook was their hostility to the phrase 'knowing Jesus personally'. Like it made them angry. But, Sid, surely… if you do know Jesus personally – immediately, directly – you couldn't take exception to it being said. When I was a teenager, I fell in with a crowd of born-again Spirit-filled Jesus freaks, at a time when I was on my first round of anti-depressants, drowning in lostness and despair, and they said if I opened my heart to Jesus and invited him in, he would come in to

83 John 13:35.
84 1 John 4:20 NLT.

me and be my Lord and save me. I wanted that. I'd reached a dead end. I'd reached the stage of collapsing sobbing in shop doorways. I needed *someone* to save me. So I did what they said. I did ask him in to my heart. And he did save me. I was well again, and happy. My soul filled up with a radiance of joy. Gosh, that was more than forty years ago, and in between then and now I've been through all manner of rough times and sorrow. I've been ill and despairing and depressed and confused and terrified; but all the way through, Jesus has been with me. And every single time – *every single time*, Sid – I've reached out for him and whispered his name and asked for his help, I've been able to feel him there.

"Well, now, the thing is, a person has a vibe, don't they? When I was a schoolgirl, my best friend Helen wore glasses – extremely myopic. But she never wore them until she arrived at school and had to do her lessons, not because she was vain but because she needed a blurry world to ease her into the day. She felt she could do without close-up detail first thing in the morning. So faces were just vague roundish shapes to her. Like that man in the Bible with his eyesight half-healed who said the people looked like trees walking about.[85] But she said she always knew when it was me walking towards her, because she recognized the expression on my face. Now, I think that's really interesting. It means there's something about a person – a demeanour, a vibe, a presence – more than their features. Something even a half-blind person can see. That thing you recognize when they walk towards you is the *who* of that individual. What's particularly them and not anyone else. And I may be deluding myself – I've wondered over and over if I am – but I think there is a vibe to the presence of Jesus that I can detect, identify. It's a matter not of belief, exactly, but experience. *I can feel him there.* And that's what I mean by knowing him personally. The Jesusness of Jesus is as distinctive as the Sidness of Sid. It's nothing to do with me being self-obsessed or getting into a corner for my own insular

85   Mark 8:24.

nooky little religion. That's not it at all. In fact, if anything, walking alongside Jesus as close as I can get is the main thing that makes social encounters a viable option for me. I guess I'm the other way round from that thing in the Bible. In my case, it's more like 'How can I love the people I can see unless I love the God I cannot see.' They go together all right, but in my soul the order reverses."

"OK." Sid is draining the pasta now, dotting butter onto it, and a lavish grinding of aromatic black pepper. "So… how would you describe it? The vibe of Jesus?"

He doles the pasta out on their plates, and the sauce he has made. He reaches past Rosie for the basil in its pot on the windowsill, garnishing each plateful with a scattering of the tender green leaves. Their fragrance rises like incense. "Here you are, my Rosie," he says, passing her plate to where she is sitting at the kitchen table. She looks down at the delicious supper with appreciation. This is part of Sid loving her. Being wrapped every day in Sid's love is one of the dearest joys of her life.

"Thank you," she says. "That smells so tasty. Thank you so much."

As he flicks around the room tidying things away before he sits down to eat, she tells him: "The vibe of Jesus, above all, is a sense of warmth. Like the warmth of a mother cat or a towel from the radiator or wool that's soft and rough at the same time. I feel courage in Jesus, and hope and peace, reassurance and love. And a sort of challenge – almost a sternness – like he expects something of me. But above all, this warmth."

Sid nods, listening. He has restored the room to peaceable order.

"Shall we have a glass of red wine with that?" he asks. Then he smiles. "And maybe a small piece of bread."

For sharing and wondering

- Would you describe yourself more as an introvert or an extrovert? Why?

- What is your instinctive immediate response to the idea of "knowing Jesus personally"?
- Can you think of an encounter in your own life where you felt you did truly catch a glimpse of the love of God in another person?

Into the Mystery

Thank you for loving us, Father God. You made us, you know us intimately, and your love reaches out to save our souls and heal our hearts. Help us every day to grow in faith and wisdom. Take us by the hand and lead us on. Guide our steps in the path of freedom, the heart-knowledge of the hidden love of God.

41

Ordinary Time – Getting Inside the Light

After eight years of it, Sid is used to this.

There's Rosie, sitting on the back door step, gazing intently at something (what?) just to her left. For a long time. Not moving. She isn't reading anything, listening to anything, eating anything. Just looking. At… what? Sid wonders whether to join her. Or not. Will his presence be welcome? Intrusive? The questions of love. Am I necessary? Is this helpful?

Years ago, someone he esteemed and held dear said to Sid a thing he never forgot. This was in respect of the Syro-Phoenician woman who followed Jesus along the road, calling after him to help her. A demon afflicted her daughter. She didn't know what else to do.[86] Sid's friend observed: "Jesus walked, and he stopped. What is the speed of love?"[87] From this, Sid gleaned something about how perceptive love is: alert, responsive, insightful. And – slow. Love is, yes, quick to respond, but moves slowly. Or so it seems to him. And this is why he watches Rosie, but hesitates before presuming upon her solitude. But he does want to know – whatever is she looking at? So, moving quietly, not intruding upon her with bustle, but sitting down with Quakerly peace at her side, he enters her silence. Companionable.

86   Matthew 15:22–28 (also Mark 7:25–30).
87   The question here attributed to Sid's friend was in reality asked of his class by the Revd Canon Martin Baddeley, then principal of the Southwark Ordination Course.

A Quaker meeting begins with the first person who enters the room and sits down. Stroke of genius, that. It trains Friends to recognize the reverential space of silence, and Sid eases himself into the sphere of another's fully radiating concentration.

After a bit, she says: "I'm starting to be able to get back inside, Sid."

The response this produces in Sid's mind is more nearly allied to a question mark than to any kind of linear thought process. So he abides in silence. Best policy. He just waits. There must surely be more to come.

She turns her head and glances at him, then looks down the garden towards the great ash trees that watch over their home like guardian angels.

"The thing is, I can remember where I came from before I was here. Before I was born. I can remember the world of light. Spaciousness. Glory. In my childhood years, it hovered about me still like a bright fog; something limitless and full of hope and love. But as time went on, as I acquired knowledge and responsibilities, I felt myself becoming ever more entangled in the here and now. By my late thirties, I had become enmeshed, held fast. Once I reached my forties, I filled my world entirely with… I suppose you might say, errands. Obligations. Things I must read, do, buy, clean, cook, organize, complete, attend to, achieve. It was as though my life came fully into the material realm. Certainly my commitments and preoccupations were moral and purposeful. The church, family, my job; Sid, these forces were digesting me! Trapped in their systemic guts, I no longer looked up or looked out. Only two things remained of what had formerly been: an intense longing – a kind of grieving – and an absolute need for light. I could live only in houses with fireplaces, big, low windows – homes that I could feel surely filling with light each morning with the rising day.

"I kept leaving things. Leaving church communities, leaving jobs. Wandering off. My heart muttered 'Not this, not this… *neither is this*

Thou…'[88] Everything turned out to be painted boxes, so promising at first but empty on the inside. I heard things said about truth, vision and holiness, and my heart leapt. But on investigation it always turned out the same. Suppers and socializing, committees and administration, the curation of an accumulated hoard. It was like scraping off tar, so clinging was their friendliness and need. But I did get free.

"And as I came into my mid-fifties, I resolved to do whatever it took to find it again. The material world is like the wardrobe portal into Narnia.[89] If you focus on it with absolute pure concentration, you can pass through it into the reality that emanates it. Then every tiniest ant, carrying its mote of wood to the city, shines with utter charm. You can enter the light of the sunbeam, swim naked into the dizzying beauty of light – which has fragrance and flavour, personality, playfulness, joy.

"It took me ages. I had to hack away at the accretions of the years – possessions, commitments, affiliations, regrets, guilts, grudges, presuppositions, doctrines, self-image, worry, bad diet, the desire to be included, to belong. All of that had to go – and sometimes I almost despaired; it seemed to be taking forever. I could never get near enough, low enough, small enough, simple enough, to be so free inside that I could get inside the sunshine again, and touch the wonder and delight of a creature, a tree, a blade of grass, a cloud. But eventually, as I stuck at it, I began to recover glimpses, like partial revelations or tantalizing echoes. A snatch of… something… the merest dazzlement of a shine of… what?

"Sid, sometimes, when I sit watching, quieter and quieter, entering in, I think Jesus passes by. Not Jesus the construct, I mean – the jointed jigsaw Jesus animated by jealous dogma and anxious exclusivism. The free Jesus whose being breathes the air of the hills and the Sea of Galilee, who can sleep through the storm with his

88   St Augustine of Hippo.
89   Reference to C. S. Lewis's children's story, *The Lion, the Witch and the Wardrobe.*

head on a cushion[90] because he carries the peace of creation at the core of his being.

"When that happens, the unmistakable distinctive warmth of his presence – such gravity, such laughter, such confidence and earthy peace – I in no wise try to cling to him. But sometimes I reach out to touch the hem of his garment; and power goes out from him, and healing comes into me.

"What I want, Sid, is to be completely one with that light and beauty – merged, integrated, inextricably and irrevocably blended and intrinsically absorbed. I am hungry for the reality that lies beyond all form and appearance, but makes itself curiously known in fur and breeze, in a juicy peace, in sunlight dappling through leaves, in the tumbling of a mountain stream and the first twilight appearing of the evening star. That's what I want, Sid. So ravenously."

Sid frowns. The glimmer of a long-forgotten poem tickles the edge of his memory. Ah! George Meredith!

> *The lover of life holds life in his hand*
> *As the hills hold the day…*
> *The lover of life sees the flame in our dust*
> *And a gift in our breath.*[91]

The poet's moment of pure inspiration stumbled upon in the midst of interminably histrionic romanticism. And it was Meredith who spoke of birdsong in the same terms as Rosie is speaking now. A yearning for something lost – *"Once I was part of the music I heard… My heart shot into the breast of the bird."*[92] A regrettable image, Sid always thought – kind of violent. Destructive. But meant for the same impulse as Rosie is describing – the leaping forth of the soul, reaching beyond itself to make contact with something sublime; searching for consummation, communion. Sid wonders if this is mysticism.

90 Mark 4:38.
91 George Meredith, "In the Woods", 1887.
92 George Meredith, *Youth In Age.*

And then, this September afternoon, he shocks himself.

"Would you like a cup of tea?" he hears his own voice asking. What travesty is this? Banal. Inconsequential. The struggling into words of an inadequacy so out of its depths that he cannot meet the soul's hunger he sees and knows full well. She will hate him now, for sure. What has he broken? This will be irretrievable.

But when she turns her face back to look at him, her eyes are crinkling with laughter.

"Why, yes, Sid, I would! That would be perfect," she replies. "However, did you know?"

Because, deep down, she can see he understands.

For sharing and wondering

- Share a memory from your childhood.
- Choose a poem that beautifully puts into words your outlook on life.
- Describe some of the challenges and the joys of a close relationship in your life – perhaps a family member or a friend.

Into the Mystery

We lift up our hearts, God of power and mystery and glory, we lift up our hearts to you. We give you thanks for your glory and majesty that completes us and fills us with hope and joy. Thank you for the chance to know you, to worship you; thank you for your Holy Spirit outpoured on all humanity.

42

Ordinary Time – Last Seen Eating Dandelion Leaves

There are 143 messages in Sid's email inbox. He thinks he hasn't got the hang of this somehow. For one thing he has inadvertently signed up for the maximum notification category of two social networking sites that he rarely visits anyway; the level of communication this generates is staggering.

There's a lot of spam, too. Ads for what's euphemistically termed "Vigara" – or is that just a brand name or a spelling mistake? Urgent calls to sign petitions to save prisoners from certain death, rescue the rainforest, the elephants and some desperately unfortunate dogs in Thailand. Out-of-date reminders of past Quaker working parties and discussion groups. And some unknown individuals – Andrea, Sharon and Trixie – determined to show him a good time and share with him their intimate photographs.

And then he has all these emails from Rosie. It's sentimentality really, he realizes – but her messages are precious to him. He reads them again... but can't bring himself to press "Delete". Because it was from Rosie. Her mind. Her love. Her connection.

As he works his way through, employing an increasingly slash-and-burn approach, he notices a "1" up at the top where it says Inbox.

He looks for the new message – from Rosie, who has taken her laptop to a spot of sunshine near the window on this day of storm and wind.

Sid smiles. The subject line says, "Hoorya!" Rosie's emails are peppered with typos. He opens it.

> **Hi honey,** it says. **I weighed myself this morning – whoop! whoop! – I've lost two stones this year! Have you noticed? Do I look different? Am I beautiful?** (This last in tiny letters.)

Sid clicks the tab to reply, and stops to think. Sid likes email conversations, even with all the nonsense of writing to someone who is actually in the same house. It gives him time to weigh his words and frame a reply that says what he means. Editing is a luxury withheld from face-to-face conversation. And being alone gives Rosie the freedom and boldness to say what she otherwise might not. She wouldn't normally ask for reassurance that she is beautiful, nor admit to losing weight on purpose.

> **Yes, I have noticed,** he types. **Can I buy you a new outfit to celebrate, in case you get lost in the woolly folds of last year's sweater? You do indeed look different – but don't worry; you are still beautiful. In fact you look so different I think perhaps you deserve a new name. Hmm. What shall it be? Let me see... To have lost so much weight, you must have been subsisting on ozone and morning dew. Perhaps we can have your name changed – by deed poll, if you like – from Rosie Ashley to Ariel Rutz.**

He imagines Rosie smiling. The orchid in the bathroom is a constant worry to her. Has it got enough water? Too much? Does it need feeding? Its inhospitable compost made primarily from chopped bark, and its questing aerial roots, perplex and amaze her. How can a plant like that stay alive? How can it bloom forth in such a splendour of perfect flowers? She makes sure to give it rain water, not the denatured stuff from the tap that smells of chemicals; that way at least she hopes it can glean the nutrients it needs.

New mail has dropped into his inbox.

Sustenance derived without clinging, it says. **Sitting light to the material plane. Oh, Sid, to this I aspire! I suspect that much sin and sorrow is really about being stuck in the mud. Wanting what other people have. Fighting for power and possession of the land. Expansion of empire, the desire for ownership, the greed for more. Holding onto things, resisting change, acquisitiveness. Wanting to keep and control. Holding on. Trying to stay young, to attract, to possess, to keep. Like the old marriage vows – "to have and to hold" – SID! NOOOOOOO! Only to love! To live with an open hand, to share and let be. To allow the wild things free passage and the small weeds a place to grow. Down with the concrete, the corporation and the gun! So long as humanity joins forces with Mammon to enslave and consume, I shall move on, move on, move on... higher up the mountain... looking for quietness, fresh air and birdsong. Looking for clear streams and real peace, the scent of the black spruce and the frankincense tree perched on its outcrop. They will say of me, "Last seen eating dandelion leaves" and "look for her higher up, in the Land of the Sunrise". Eventually, like Jesus, I will disappear into the clouds. Not bad for a fleshy urban houseplant, eh?**

And another email.

Ariel Rutz!! Hahahaha!!!

Then:

Yes please! (about the new outfit).

In a book called *Nothing Left Over*,[93] Sid once read these words: "Problems arise where things accumulate." The author proposed the view that all illnesses – indeed most of life's bad scenarios – come about as a result of accumulation. When Sid turns the idea over in his mind and probes it, he concludes it to be true. Too much acid in the body. Too much sugar, too much fat, too much inertia. Then, too much territory and too much power accumulating in the hands of too few. Huge corporations, superpowers. Growth

---

93 *Nothing Left Over: A Plain and Simple Life,* by Toinette Lippe, published by Monkfish Book Publishing Company.

economics. Greed. Clutter in homes offering shelter to dirt and mould, generating lethargy and hopelessness. Mounting personal overdrafts and public debt. Overcrowding and traffic congestion. Fly-tipping. Factory farming. Pollution. Overpopulation. Yes. Problems arise where things accumulate. He reflects that learning to disperse and dispense with stuff is a necessary art for today. What was that thing he read... made a note of? He hunts through the spilling riot of papers on his desk. (Problems arise where things accumulate – ha! Surely not.) Jottings scattered and piled, hoards of the mind. This, scribbled down in haste, from the Bible – "give me neither poverty nor riches, but give me only my daily bread. Otherwise, I may have too much and disown you and say, 'Who is the Lord?' Or I may become poor and steal, and so dishonour the name of my God."[94] No, it wasn't that. Ah, yes – here: "The skill of this century is editing."[95] The wisdom of judicious cutting back. Life flowers when pruned.

Sid contemplates, for one fleeting moment, teasing Rosie about her ready acceptance of his offer to buy her a new outfit. Isn't that accumulation? But, no. It's never wise to push people who live close to the edge, not even in play.

So he simply writes back:

> **We'll hit the shops first thing in the morning. I was thinking of making a cup of tea. Can I interest you in some water and a lettuce leaf?**

For sharing and wondering

- Think of two quotes to share, that you have found especially insightful.

94 Proverbs 30:8–9 NIV.
95 Graham Hill, founder of TreeHugger.com – in an interview with faircompanies. com, he says: "We really have a culture of excess... we're not any happier and what you'll see again and again are people who really cut back and really edit their lives will find themselves much happier. They have more mental clarity. They end up having more time and it's often better financially." http://faircompanies.com/blogs/view/lifeedited-cut-space-stuff-media-friends-and-be-happier/

- What have you kept and treasured – texts in your phone memory, letters, photos, gifts – as mementos of people you specially love?

- Clutter. Is it a problem in your home? Or do you live clutter-free?

Into the Mystery

In your service, O Lord, is perfect freedom. Under the reign of your Spirit, we find liberty. Transform us, remake us, set us free from everything that compromises and mars the beauty and truth you made us to express.

43

Ordinary Time – Perfect Storm

"What?" says Sid. "What is it?"

He knows that look on Rosie's face. Hard to put it into words. It's like the swell of the sea, a dark tide of sorrow on a night of no moon. Stillness without hope. Keeping that expression at bay is part of what Sid considers to be his life's purpose.

"What's the matter, Rosie?" he asks her.

"I'm thinking," she says, "about perfect storm. With reference to climate change. Did you know, Sid, that John Beddington – and, for heaven's sake, he was once the chief scientific advisor for England, so he ought to know – said that by the year 2030 the conditions would be in place to create a perfect storm. A convergence of climate, energy and economic crises. That means… Sid that means a few more years of escalating war, violent weather, famine and disease – and after that the stew will really hit the fan. Perfect storm. I'm frightened, Sid. I go on steadily with life as usual, because what else can you do? But underneath the quiet rhythm of the everyday is this dreadful cold fear. Old age is hard, Sid. I've worked in nursing homes and hospitals, I've seen what cancer and dementia can do to people. I've seen the struggles of increasing frailty, the creaky old bones, the pain of arthritis and the dental problems, the failing eyesight, the increasing deafness. Isn't that bad enough? Gradually losing everything – isn't that as much as a person can cope with even if there is support and medicine and surgery? Even when someone is safe and warm and fed, it's not easy growing old, Sid. It's not easy to die. But what will our old age be like? What kind of death awaits us? Perfect storm. I'm frightened, Sid."

Sid listens. He doesn't know what to say. He has read the journals, searched online, paid attention to the discussions. He knows the score. Sid is all too well aware that unprecedented planetary emergency has crossed the horizon and is already, unstoppably, beginning to take shape. And he knows that governments worldwide, locked into short-termism and pressured on every side, have no intention of planning the carbon emission curbs that could even start to put a dent into the approaching Armageddon.

Rosie doesn't look at him. She is gazing into the chasm of an impossible, unbearable future.

"I see people online – on the social networks," she says, "saying all this is good because it means Jesus is coming again. They see no reason to change a thing. The Arctic can melt. The Amazon can be razed. Goodo and hurry up, Lord. They don't know what they're saying, they're like dreamers talking in their sleep. These are the same people who feel sorry for themselves if they have a headache, and think it's unacceptable to be given smooth peanut butter when you wanted crunchy. Are they ready to face a world without water or complete economic collapse?

"And then I've read long, detailed articles about stockpiling food. The importance of having a big garden to grow your own vegetables, the necessity for storing cans and jars and seeds and flour for the future. They aren't thinking straight. Two things drive a coach and horses straight through that bright idea. The first is: what kind of person would you be if you tucked into your tins of beans while your neighbour starved to death or cooked his own dog to feed his family? The second is, what makes anybody think a scenario could possibly exist in which one farsighted family had enough to get by while all their less organized neighbours looked on and said 'Dang! I wish we'd thought of that'? The whole thing would disintegrate into looting and gun violence, terror and killing and every man for himself. Call me an infidel but, for me, saying, 'Look on the bright side, the Rapture must be any time soon,' doesn't quite cut it."

And now she looks him straight in the eye, and Sid, who has volunteered in hospice and on Quaker listening groups, recognizes the look of the trapped animal, the soul faced with what must not, cannot, be happening; but is.

"Rosie," he says, and instantly something eases in her. Because they have each other. Because Sid is gentle, and kind. Because they belong to one another. Rosie has thought many times and now, again, today – if we can face this together it will not be as bad (whatever it is) as if we have to go through it alone.

"Yes," he says, "I think it may be very bad; as indeed for so many people in every time and place it already has been and is. We have lived a charmed life, my love. Housed and fed, employed, a health service, a democracy, a temperate climate, employment, times of peace. OK, we've both had our struggles, but the terrors of torture and rape, famine and foul water, war and broad-scale natural disaster have passed us by. Life has been good; but we can no more expect than any human being that it will always be so. What you and I face is terrifying; but so was the prospect before prisoners brought to the wheel, the rack, the fire, the iron maiden and the brazen bull. The human race has done this to the Earth, and they have always been hell-bent upon turning on one another. We are a cruel species. Perhaps the perfect storm began the day God breathed life into Adam. But... there's the story in the Gospels about a terrible storm. And Jesus was asleep. When they woke him up, he spoke peace, and they were saved."[96]

"I know." Rosie's voice is flat and despondent. "I know the story. But Jesus isn't here now and he can't save us from this."

Sid nods, thoughtfully. "Well," he says, "you might like to think about that a bit more. For one thing, I believe – and I think you do

96 See Mark 4:35–41 and Matthew 8:23–27.

as well, really – Jesus *is* here now. He is with us, in the power of the resurrection. We can call on him today just as really and literally as his friends in the boat on Galilee. And about saving us – well, save us from what? Rosie, everyone must face adversity, and everyone has to die. Nobody dies of anything nice. Planet Earth is a living being as much as you and I are. Sooner or later it had to happen. Eventually, she would get sick and die. The sun is cooling, the universe is expanding. The circumstances permitting life are a brief extraordinary miracle of coincidence. And it is over.

"But even though I am as scared as you are, I still do really believe that Jesus is with us, and that he can transform this perfect storm wherever he is invited to. The world doesn't want his intervention; the world by and large thinks Jesus can push off. But for the storm inside you and the storm inside me – and those are the only areas where we have any responsibility or authority – he can speak peace, and work his miracle for this present moment. The thing is, Rosie, we have to wake him up."

She looks at him, and he sees the smallest beginning of a smile.

"Waking up Jesus," she says. "That would be… rousing compassion, the spirit of self-sacrifice, the willingness to let the buck stop with me."

"Yes." He takes her hand. "Healing, faith, forgiveness, understanding, prayer, trust – all those things. How could that not change everything? Jesus… well, Jesus was crucified and nothing stopped that happening. But it was the means of the reconciliation of all creation to the living God. Perfect love for a perfect storm. Rosie, let's make a pact, you and I. From this day on, whatever storms befall us – the perfect one or the regular ordinary sort – let's commit to the practice that when things get too much we will wake up Jesus: 'Help, Lord! We are drowning!' And keep an open mind as to what he might be able to do."

For sharing and wondering

- What do we mean when we pray "Thy kingdom come on earth as it is in heaven"?
- We may not be able to solve all the problems of climate change, but what small, individual things could we do for the animals, birds, trees, insects or waterways of our neigbourhood?
- Think of a time in your life when you found it difficult to put your trust in Jesus, but he didn't let you down.

Into the Mystery

We thank you for the providence and grace that watch over our lives, God of love. Help us to trust you in every circumstance of life. Help us to be sensible and prudent, and yet still to delight in the fleeting joy, in the unique blessings of this day. Help us to remember that no imagined future is ever going to be real, that our way into realistic hope will always be through the door of this present moment opening in to your unfailing love.

44

Feast of St Francis of Assisi

When two middle-aged people get married, it's a tricky thing to adjust. Habits are formed, assumptions and expectations established.

When Sid and Rosie got together, there was the complicated issue of the sleeping arrangements. Rosie, like all right-thinking people, has a profound affection and appreciation for her pocket-sprung, silk-and-wool, very expensive mattress, her 13.5-tog duvet and the four soft and accommodating pillows that receive her reclining form when she tucks in with a good book at the end of the day. And Sid sleeps on the floor, under one blanket.

He was put up to this uncompromising and angular habit by avid reading about Gandhi at an impressionable age. Nobody was allowed to make common cause with the Mahatma unless they acquiesced to eating simply, dressing simply, getting up early, sharing all the housework – and sleeping on the floor.

About the same time Sid discovered and fell hook, line and sinker for St Francis, he also got into Gandhi, in a big way; and has slept on the floor ever since.

Today, the feast of St Francis, Sid gets up early as usual – before sunrise, now the days are drawing in – and when Rosie opens one eye on the chilly morning, it is to see him sitting quietly on his patch of floor, looking at the candle he's lit.

She goes downstairs to make cups of tea, bringing one up for Sid before climbing back into bed with hers. He smiles, taking the mug's comforting heat between his hands.

"The great strength of St Francis – I think," he says, "is his odd propensity for taking things literally. In general I am very wary of people who take things literally – especially the Bible. But in the case of St Francis, I think it was his secret."

Sid takes a cautious sip of his tea. It's still too hot really, so he gives it a minute and goes on talking. Rosie, regally recumbent on her heaped pillows, listens placidly.

"When the still, small voice came to him, with the instructions: 'Go out and build my house, for it is nearly falling down,' Francis looked for stones not metaphors. He had this childlike spirit, innate simplicity, that started with the obvious and worked inwards. That's what made him a revolutionary. He didn't think twice and he didn't try to spiritualize his visions. He got up and got on with things."

Rosie thinks of these early conversations as evening-in-the-morning – a luxury of those who work from home and retired folk. An hour or two at the day's beginning when the mind is still expanded from the astral landscape of dreams; special talking time. She sips her tea (hers is Earl Grey, his is English Breakfast), turning over in her mind the possibilities of literalism, distinctly remembering proposing this to Sid herself – about our bodies being temples of the Holy Spirit. He seems to have forgotten.

The warm halo of candlelight still illuminates Sid's thinking face, as the first light of day lifts away the shadows of night.

"When it comes to the words of Jesus Christ in the Gospels," he continues, "we have a bad habit of spiritualizing them."

"Spiritualizing Jesus?" Rosie thinks she will string him along. "Is that possible?"

"Well, I believe so."

"Example?"

Sid frowns, considering. "One time he said, 'Whoever has will be given more, and they will have an abundance. Whoever does not have, even what they have will be taken from them.'[97] I grew up understanding that as a threat – something along the lines of 'be productive, or else!' But then I began to notice that it's kind of political – it's the way of the world. Like, rich people can afford to bulk-buy and bulk-store and have cars to ferry their stuff home; so they can get their groceries cheaper than poor people who have no car, small homes with little storage space, weekly wages or pensions and no savings. If you take what he says metaphorically, it's a threat about the day of judgment. But if you take it literally, it can be compassionate, it can be political, it can be psychological, fiscal – *useful*.

"Another thing he said was, 'those of you who do not give up everything you have cannot be my disciples.'[98] Wait – what? He said *what?* I mean, Rosie, who have you ever met who's even *tried* to do that? Oh, there are a few visionaries and monastics who've made the shift to corporate ownership, making the compromise that owning things communally is the same as giving them up. But most of us just think 'Really?' and give it no further consideration. Hardly any preachers will touch it with a bargepole. Those that do, usually take up the task of explaining, since he couldn't possibly have meant that he must have meant something else. But, the one or two who have tried it – and St Francis was one of that tiny few – well, they set the world ablaze. I think, he meant it literally.

"And then there's the business about the bed. You remember? The paralysed man? They let him down through the roof to Jesus, who told him his sins were forgiven. And that started up the same old argument with the religious types, ending in Jesus telling the man to take up his bed and walk.[99]

"Well, now, Thoreau picks up that text in his book about the year he spent living in a shed on the shores of Walden Pond. He speaks about how encumbered people get with belongings, likening us to butterflies caught in a spider's web or muskrats caught in a

97 Matthew 13:12, NIV – see also Matthew 25:29 and Luke 19:26.
98 Luke 14:33 NIV.
99 John 5:8.

trap, unable to get away, 'in a dead set' as he put it, hemmed in by possessions. He said 'It would surpass the powers of a well man nowadays to take up his bed and walk, and I should certainly advise a sick one to lay down his bed and run.'[100]

"What if we took Jesus literally? What if we tackled the sicknesses of our society with plain living and exercise, walking, and sleeping on the floor? Our health would improve a thousand-fold, and we'd be more flexible, less hemmed in – less *paralysed* by stuff and possessions and easy living. The bed's a good example. Why, we even say 'go to bed', not 'go to sleep'! Fixtures have taken over our lives, making us need bigger houses, bigger incomes. And these things have the seeds of war, because the more you need the more you're looking around to see how you can get it and who to get it from. Furniture needs *territory* – it can't move.

"If people would just give it a try – a year, say – taking Jesus literally. My God! There'd be a revolution! Freedom! Health! Wellbeing! Peace! Flexibility! If we could only stop spiritualizing everything, and just do it."

He falls silent. The day has come. The sun is fully risen. He drinks his tea, half-cold by now. Rosie has long since finished hers, and swings her legs out of bed, sliding her feet into her fluffy slippers and reaching for her dressing gown. She smiles at him.

"Sid Ashley," she says, "taking the as-if out of Jesus since the 1960s."

Sid leans forward to blow out the candle, wanting to hide from her sight the frown and flush of irritation he can't help. But she sees.

"I'm not being sarcastic, Sid," she tells, him, love in her voice, reaching down to lay her hand on his head as she passes on her way to the bathroom. "Gandhi, St Francis, Jesus – are they not the lights of the world? But I thought you told me people who take the Bible literally are a confounded nuisance; start wars and things."

He looks crestfallen. "Well, yes. I did. But this is different."

---

100 Henry David Thoreau, *Walden*, chapter 1.

For sharing and wondering

- Think of an example of something in the Bible you feel should be taken literally, and something that should not?
- In what ways do your beliefs influence the everyday detail of your life – for example how you shop, what you eat, how you dress, how you furnish your home, what you watch on TV?
- Think of someone you have met or read about, who was led to make a big change in their life as a result of awakening spiritual belief.

Into the Mystery

In every day, in every choice, in every step we make, breathe into our lives, O Lord our God. Fill us with your vision, illumine us with your mind, may your holiness and goodness shape us according to the beauty of your love.

45

Feast of St Michael and All Angels

Rosie comes downstairs wearing the green fleece gilet she went up to fetch. The summer stretched out long and golden, but there's a chill in the air now, and the breeze is fresher. The grass is heavy with cold dew in the early mornings, and the mist lies in the hollows. Here and there in the garden, exuberant sprays of Michaelmas daisies, lilac petals and gold centres, show beautiful splashes of colour. The year is turning.

"Sid?" In the kitchen he is getting carrots and apples out of the fridge, cutting them up to make their breakfast juice. "It's the twenty-seventh today. Wasn't it... haven't we had the equinox?"

"We have. It was on the twenty-third this year. It's usually on the twenty-third or the twenty-second – can be on the twenty-fourth. It depends. The Roman calendar – the Gregorian calendar – 365 days to the year, thirty or thirty-one days to the month, doesn't quite accommodate to the rhythms of the planets, the Earth's relationship to the sun and the moon. The Romans were less interested in ebb and flow, light and darkness, waxing and waning moons, and more into mathematics and systems. It made them formidable political rulers, I guess, but their religion was a bit... tidy. Their houses, you know, it's a funny thing: when they came to England, the Anglo-Saxons lived in small huts, in villages. The Romans arrived and built their villas with heating running under the mosaic floor and plumbing – grand, sophisticated places; palaces by comparison. You'd have thought the Anglo-Saxons would have embraced that way of living with eager arms. Not a bit of it. The Romans came – *veni, vidi, vici* – and they went, and the Anglo-Saxons left their lovely villas empty, let the earth reclaim the stones the Romans had quarried. People making kids' history books think it was because the Romans were so much cleverer and the Anglo-Saxons were too primitive to emulate them, but that's not it. They had different values is all.

"So anyway – yes, we had the equinox. Why? Sorry, I'm going to put the machine on now, it'll make a hell of a noise for a minute. Talk to me after."

He flicks the switch and their state-of-the-art masticating Champion juicer springs to life, grinding and pulping. Sid feeds the pulp through, and again, until what's left is minimal and almost dry. He divides the bright orange juice between the two glasses ready on the table, rinses all the juicing parts meticulously, dries them, oils and reassembles the thing, and sits down at the table with Rosie to enjoy their drinks replete with vitamins and enzymes, fresh and delicious.

Rosie concentrates on the taste of her juice for a moment, then goes back to where she left off.

"The equinox – it's one of the Celtic festivals, isn't it? But which one?"

"Mabon. The time of the second harvest, so a thanksgiving. You know – 'all is safely gathered in'. Not much is said about it because it speaks for itself. In rural communities – settled, farming communities with fruits and grains as well as flocks – nothing, but nothing, is bigger than harvest festival. My uncle Joe was a farmer, and he regarded himself as a regular churchgoer; he went every year without fail, at harvest festival, to give thanks for the bounty of the fields. And of course, Mabon has themes of laying by, preparation for the winter."

"Your Uncle Joe? Wasn't he a Catholic, then? Didn't he have to go to Mass every Sunday?"

"Church of England. He married my Auntie Mary. Caused a stir in the family, her marrying outside the one true faith! But it was a good marriage, for all that. They each kept to their own, when it came to church. She never missed Mass – and when we were little, it was every day, not every Sunday."

Rosie looks impressed. She drains the last drips of her juice, and wipes out the residue with her finger, licking it thoughtfully.

"So… what feast did the missionaries settle on Mabon?"

Sid smiles. "St Michael and All Angels. It comes a few days after – on 29 September. My guess is, the harvest celebration involved some serious revelry! All that mead and cider! The monks let them sober up a bit before patiently bringing their mind back to learning the gospel."

"Oh. Why did they pick St Michael for Mabon?"

"It's in the Bible. Jesus and his parables: 'The harvest is the end of the world; and the reapers are the angels.'[101] And the angel of the Revelation, saying, 'Thrust in thy sickle, and reap: for the time is come for thee to reap; for the harvest of the earth is ripe.'[102] It's clever, because in the teaching of Jesus, the harvest is a metaphor for the end times – judgment, final reckoning. Eschatological – death, heaven, hell, accounting for yourself. And Mabon is about getting the crops in, storing, thanksgiving, plenteousness – 'the valleys stand so thick with corn that even they are singing'[103] – but it's also got a sombre note, a black thread, about the days of cold and winter ahead, and getting ready.

"So the feast of St Michael and All Angels is a two-in-one celebration of harvest and warning about the last judgment and the harvest of souls. Is your life good fruit and wholesome grain? Are you ready?"

101 Matthew 13:39.
102 Revelation 14:15.
103 Quoted from W. Chatterton Dix's hymn "To Thee, O Lord, our hearts we raise".

"Oh, yes!" Rosie chips in. "The anthroposophists – the Rudolf Steiner people with the lovely schools and handcrafts, storytelling and spinning and wonderful toys for children – they keep the feast of St Michael and All Angels. They say St Michael stands pointing down the year towards the coming of the Christ child in the depths of the year's night. He's pointing to Jesus, but he's also saying, 'The dark days are coming! Get ready!'

Sid nods. "Yep. That's the one. It's interesting, because it's not a jolly feast, which is kind of surprising at harvest thanksgiving. It's very challenging. I wonder if that's why it comes several days after Mabon as well as giving them a chance to get the booze out of their systems – maybe right on the celebration, folks aren't in such a mood to hear about Last Things. Killjoy, you know?"

"Sid – do you believe in angels?"

"I do. For sure. Don't you?"

"I think so. I mean, the angels in the Bible, they got there from the Zoroastrian influences, didn't they? The legions of Ahura Mazda ranged against the hosts of Angra Mainyu. The sense of a whole cosmos, physical and spiritual, drawn up into battle lines. And I don't believe in that. I'm with Isaiah and Abraham – the Lord our God, the Lord is One. There is no power but God. I'm not sure I believe in the devil, either. And yet, there is a force… a force of darkness that seems almost personal. And the sense of a kindred that watches over us. And people have seen angels too – the angels at Mons in World War I, and angels standing guard over missionaries and nuns. Yes. Yes, I think I do believe in angels.

"Sid – your juice is heavenly. D'you fancy some toast now?"

For sharing and wondering

- What is your favourite time of year, and why?
- What do you think about angels?
- What five things would make a home happy, for you?

Into the Mystery

You speak to us through the seasons, Creator God; the mountains and stars, the sunlight and the sea reveal your glory. Help us to find the time to walk in nature in your company, to lose ourselves in wonder at all the beauty you have made, to delight in sunset and dawn, in cloudscapes and frost and rain.

46

Feast of St Teresa of Ávila

"Sid," says Rosie, looking up from the book she's reading on her Kindle, "do you think it matters what path you walk?"

Sid laughs. "Well, of course it does, you nana! If you walk the wrong path you'll end up in the wrong place, won't you?"

"But will you?" Rosie persists. "Is it like that? How can you know, really, where the path you are on will take you? I mean, the paths through life aren't *marked*, are they? And even when they are – that time we set out to explore the McArthur Glen Retail Village at Ashford – do you remember? We selected it on the satnav and set off, and then after about fifteen minutes it seemed to be taking us a very strange route to Ashford. And you glanced at the navigation panel and saw it said we had 327 miles still to go. When you pulled over to investigate it turned out I'd selected a place in Edinburgh. It's the same with life paths. You find one with 'JESUS' written on it and you think, 'Oh, Jesus – that'll be going my way, then.' So you start walking along that path and find yourself all tangled up with a gang of people arguing and fighting and blaming each other, straitjacketed into rules and prohibitions and insisting on doing everything their own way. You decide to try a different path at the next crossroads.

"So you see a sign onto a different road that says simply 'Peace', and you think that sounds lovely. As you walk along you discover 'Peace' is another name for Islam, and before you know it you're jostling along with a crowd of folk into female circumcision and jihad, beheading people and plotting to blow up the infidel as comprehensively as possible. 'Uh-oh,' you think, 'this isn't the path for me.'

"At the very next opportunity you see a sign saying 'O house of Jacob, come, let us walk in the light of the Lord.'[104] And you feel sure that must be the way for you. But it turns out to be just another way of war and violence, with a massive apartheid wall and a history of self-pity. By this time you're about done, but you spot a quiet little lane with a sign saying 'This way to the meditation hall,' and you decide to give it one more shot. But wary now, you enquire carefully of the people walking along it: who they might be – and they tell you the name of the teacher they are following. Having your iPhone handily about your person, you look him up, only to find a bunch of websites railing against him for his sexual predations in an ashram somewhere. After that you decide not to bother with paths any more, and go for the sheep-tracks across open country and the badger-trails through the woods.

"All those paths, whatever was written on them, lead to the same place, Sid. War. But you wouldn't have known it from simply reading the signposts. You'd have thought they each went to their own place. And if you asked any of the travellers on any of the roads, they'd tell you their path is the only way to get home. It's all just one big disappointment."

Sid listens to this rant patiently. "I see," he says, when she's finished. "So when Swami Kripalu says 'There are many paths up the mountain, but there is only one mountain,' you may be thinking these roads aren't even anywhere near the mountain, they're all headed off to a battlefield somewhere in the middle of the plain?"

"That is precisely what I think," says Rosie. "So, how do you find the way?"

Sid scratches his head thoughtfully. "Whatever set you off thinking about this, anyway?"

104 Isaiah 2:5 ESV.

"I'm reading St Teresa of Ávila's book of her life. And I came across this thing she said, 'Just as there are many mansions in Heaven, there are many paths.' So I wondered what you thought about it."

Sid puffs out his cheeks, lets his breath blow out in a sigh. "Wow. I see. Well, as to St Teresa of Ávila, something she taught was to pray, always pray. And she was sufficiently audacious as to propose that people sit quietly with God, as with a dear and familiar friend. Chat with him. Tell him what's on your heart. Listen to what he has to say. Maybe that's all part of finding the right way home. And what you've read, about there being many paths – I wonder if that was good counsel about not judging other people. Not being dogmatic and saying mine is the only way. And perhaps also about not giving up. She said, 'May you not forget the infinite possibilities that are born of faith.' St Teresa was courageous and persevering. She believed in simplicity, and she always saw the funny side of things. Lightness of spirit – both not taking yourself too seriously, and not getting too attached to the things of this world – might that be a balloon ride up the mountain?"

Rosie looks disheartened, Sid perceives. So he tries again. "There's something else St Teresa said, Rosie – 'May you trust God that you are exactly where you are meant to be.' Could that be a good way to tackle things? Not even to look for paths, not to seek any kind of way; just blossom where you're planted? Like Thich Nhat Hanh the Buddhist teacher says – 'I have arrived. I am home.' Perhaps the love of Jesus can be home enough? Maybe there is no need to go on searching."

She looks at him. "Yes. I like that idea. There's this thing I jotted down that she said…"

Rosie reaches down to her notepad lying near her on the floor. "This is it. Listen:

> Let nothing disturb you,
> Let nothing frighten you,
> All things are passing away:
> God never changes.

Patience obtains all things.
Whoever has God lacks nothing;
God alone suffices.

"Maybe it's what you just said. Maybe we're already home, and we just have to realize it."

"I think that could be it," says Sid. "And I've sometimes wondered, about those paths – are they in fact leading up the mountain? Might they be leading *down* the mountain, instead? Could the wisdom of the religions of the world lie not in how well their devotees are progressing on the upward slog, so much as in the light shining down, the streams of life-giving water flowing down from higher up, from the top. I'm really not sure. What do you think?"

Rosie smiles. "There's a couple more St Teresa quotes I jotted down. She said, 'All the way to heaven is heaven,' and she said, 'To reach something good, it is useful to have gone astray.' And... this... which I don't think St Teresa said at all. 'Have patience with everything unresolved in your heart and to try to love the questions themselves.' Who said that? Do you know?"

"Rainer Maria Rilke,"[105] says Sid. "It goes on: 'The point is to live everything. Live the questions now. Perhaps then, someday far in the future, you will gradually, without even noticing it, live your way into the answer.'"

For sharing and wondering

- How would you describe the path your life is taking right now, and the landscape your path is passing through.

- What are two of the questions that puzzle you and you are not able to resolve at the present time?

- Do you think you are exactly where God means you to be, at the present time, or do changes come to mind that you think it's time to tackle?

105 1903, *Letters to a Young Poet*.

Into the Mystery

Lead me, Lord, lead me in thy righteousness;
make thy way plain before my face.
For it is thou, Lord, thou, Lord only,
that makest me dwell in safety.

Samuel Wesley (1810-76)

47

St Luke's Tide

"I'm stripping the bed," says Rosie, "if you've got anything extra you want washing, apart from what's already in the basket. Put your PJs out. It's such a nice day – if it doesn't cloud over, everything should dry in this breeze and sunshine."

"St Luke's little summer," Sid says, looking out of the window.

"What?"

"It's St Luke's Tide. Yesterday – 18 October – was St Luke's Day. Every year at the time of his feast, there's a short spell of good weather. And then storms with St Jude's Day, on the twenty-eighth."

"Really? Every year? How come?"

"No idea, but apparently it's true, and it does seem to be more or less that way. A breathing space of mellow weather, and then the storms and blustery days – all the wind and rain of the back end of the year."

"Who's St Jude, anyway?" Rosie asks him as she pulls off the pillowcases.

"St Jude Thaddeus. One of the apostles. You know – wrote the epistle of St Jude."

"Oh, goodness! I forgot that even existed! I suppose I must have read it at some point, but I couldn't begin to tell you what it says."

She tosses the dirty linen into a heap by the bedroom door, and empties the few bits from the laundry basket on top of it.

"Well, it's… here, listen to this." Sid picks up the tatty old Bible from the lower shelf of his bedside unit. "'These are spots in your feasts of charity, when they feast with you, feeding themselves without fear: clouds they are without water, carried about of winds; trees whose fruit withereth, without fruit, twice dead, plucked up by the roots; Raging waves of the sea, foaming out their own shame; wandering stars, to whom is reserved the blackness of darkness for ever.'[106] Somebody must have had a sense of humour, to set his feast day at the point the winter storms begin to rage!

"And then, he goes on: 'But ye, beloved, building up yourselves on your most holy faith, praying in the Holy Ghost, keep yourselves in the love of God, looking for the mercy of our Lord Jesus Christ unto eternal life. And of some have compassion, making a difference: And others save with fear, pulling them out of the fire…'[107]

"I think it must be because of that bit they made St Jude the patron saint of desperate cases and lost causes. Brands snatched from the burning, and all that.

"So when the storms start to rage, and we batten down the hatches – wind wuthering round the rooftop, rain lashing against the window panes – it recalls to us St Jude exhorting those poor beleaguered early followers of Christ, so many of them martyred, to stand firm and not be afraid in those turbulent times. 'Earnestly contend for the faith,' he says.[108]

Rosie stands thinking, listening to the extracts as he reads them to her, the bundle of washing piled up in her arms.

"Not just then, either," she says. "Nigeria, Iraq, Bhutan, Pakistan… so many places where the Christian faith means a prison sentence or a death sentence. Harassment. Persecution. Violence and fear. Sid, I don't know what's wrong with the human race. After all, it's not as if the church itself was so very squeaky clean. Quakers and Puritans burned at the stake, Catholic and Protestant in pitched battle, homosexuals hounded and witch-hunted, pregnant girls

106 Jude 12–13.
107 Jude 20–23.
108 Jude 3.

thrown out into the street tainted with shame. Doesn't matter where you look, it seems religion gives people all the excuse they need for being really mean."

Sid nods in affirmation, closing his Bible and slipping it back into the bedside shelf. "True enough. Perhaps that's why they fixed St Luke's Tide at this little summer. St Luke was gentle."

"A healer," says Rosie.

"Yes, 'the beloved physician'.[109] But he was also the champion of what would have been known in the *Old* Testament as the *anawim*."

"The who?"

"It strictly means 'little ones', but it's all those members of society who are forgotten and unimportant, of no account. Children. Women. The poor. Ethnic minorities."

Rosie smiles. "The lowly worms."

"Absolutely! St Luke, who was a Holy Spirit fan, offers a sort of tour de force in his Gospel – and in Acts – of evidence for the presence and activity of the Holy Spirit in all those lowly worms. He stood up for them. He wanted them all to have their time in the sun. And not only that: St Luke – oh, this is the thing I love about him above all else – he refers to what most of the saved and the righteous call 'sinners' as 'the lost'."

"Not like St Jude, then! What was it you read? '... to whom is reserved the blackness of darkness for ever...'?"

"Exactly so. You know the story of the lost sheep in the Gospels? How the good shepherd leaves the ninety and nine on the hillside to go in search of the one that wanders off? When St Matthew tells the story, he says of the shepherd, 'and *if* he finds it...'[110] But not St Luke. How he tells it is, 'and *when* he finds it'.[111] St Luke's shepherd goes on searching and *never* gives up. If that's not worth a little summer, I don't know what is!"

Rosie takes her mound of laundry on down to the kitchen and

109 Colossians 4:14.
110 Matthew 18:13.
111 Luke 15:5.

loads the machine, while Sid gets his boots out of the wardrobe and laces them onto his feet.

As he follows Rosie down the stairs, he stoops to pick up a stray sock dropped unnoticed from the gathered washing. She'll be annoyed if everything else fitted into one load and just this is left over.

The lost sock, Sid thinks; a little gnarled and smelly. Must belong to St Luke, the kind physician who had a heart to search out all the lost. Unless it counts as a cause, and belongs to St Jude. Did they wear socks, I wonder, those early saints? Probably not. It isn't that old. And Rosie tells me socks look seriously sad worn with sandals.

For sharing and wondering

- What books of the Bible have you never studied, or not read for a long time, and would like to make time to discuss?
- Describe someone you know who is a really excellent advert for the Christian faith.
- Think of an example to share of a time in your life that felt like a turbulent storm, and a time that felt like a perfect summer's day.

Into the Mystery

God of love, you have room in your heart for everyone. There is no one you don't care about, no one you have forgotten. Your love never gives up, never loses hope. Help us to walk in your love, kindly and optimistically, living every day the faith that speaks of your mercy and grace.

48

Martinmas

"What shall we have for supper?" Rosie stands holding open the fridge door, and turns round, suddenly laughing. "Oh, Sid! Do you remember when Alison looked into our fridge in search of some lunch, and exclaimed in horror, 'This is all full of fruit and vegetables – there's no food in here!'"

Sid has passed on to his daughter Alison his love of cheese and Chinese takeaways. She has spent markedly less time with her father since he remarried; Sid isn't sure if it's Rosie's naturally acerbic temperament, or all the curly kale and celery, that has scared her away.

"It's the night for a feast," he answers Rosie's question. "This is a roast dinner with all the trimmings night. Pork crackling. Roast potatoes. Gravy – lots and lots of gravy."

"Why? Are you sick of dahl and brown rice or are the frosty nights whispering of fat and carbohydrate?"

"Both those things," says Sid, "and, plus – it's Martinmas."

"Today? 10th November? I thought Martinmas was on the eleventh." She shuts the fridge, and reaches for the scrap paper to make a new shopping list.

"It's the Celtic day – two for the price of one," Sid says, "because it starts at sundown. And the 10th November was the day for the big Martinmas feast. They couldn't feed all the animals through the winter cold, so they had a huge slaughter at the end of the autumn and beginning of the winter. I guess in the cold you could keep meat longer, and also of course they would have smoked the hams, but even so it was a sharing time – roast pork and roast goose for everyone.

"I think that's why they settled St Martin's Feast on it, because of the sharing. He – stop me if you've already heard this – you know about St Martin?"

"Not really," says Rosie. "I remember the Steiner people talking about Martinmas, but I don't know who he was. He… wait – is he the Roman soldier who cut his cloak in two and gave half of it to a beggar? That Martin?"

"That's the one. St Martin of Tours. It was interesting because the story says after he did that thing he saw Jesus, in a dream, telling some angels: 'Here is Martin, the Roman soldier who is not baptized; he has clothed me.' Which kind of begs the question about salvation – where does it begin? With acquiescence to a set of beliefs, or with a softened heart? Can you meet Jesus, and love him, but never know his name? Anyway, Martin was a soldier to begin with, but later he became a monk. The thing with the cloak happened early on. It was in a snowstorm, and he saw this beggar shivering in the cold. He thought the man would die without some protection from the freezing weather. He used his sword to cut his own cloak in half so they could share it. I think that's the power of the story, really – what makes it such a wise teaching. It's the pragmatism. That he didn't make an extravagant gesture, freeze to death himself to save the life of the beggar. He saw that they could both get by if the one of them who had something was willing to share. I think it says something about the power of compromise. You know, like Jim Harrison says, 'The reason to moderate is to avoid having to quit.'[112] And that thing Alfieri says at the end of *A View From the Bridge*:[113] 'Most of the time now we settle for half and I like it better.' Sharing makes life workable. Everyone wins.

112 Quoted from Jim Harrison's 2002 *Off to the Side: A Memoir*.
113 1955 play by Arthur Miller.

"So I guess the message of the early missionaries, making the hog slaughter at the start of the winter into Martinmas, was a reminder to make what they had go round – keep half and give half away."

"Oh no. Does this mean you're going to want to invite the neighbours in for dinner as well as put in your order for roast potatoes?" Rosie, incorrigibly anti-social, regards him with suspicion. "Will it do if I go online and make a donation to charity instead? Just not the real people."

Sid laughs at her. Sometimes he wonders how he ever managed to get close enough to this woman to win her heart. Nobody else does.

"Are you serious about the roast dinner, Sid?" she asks him. "I can do it if you like. But there isn't much money left in the housekeeping purse – we'll have to be careful the rest of the week if we do this today."

"Well, that'll be right on for Martinmas, too," he says.

"Because?"

"Well, after the big blow-out, they pulled their belts in. It's like a BBC action replay of Mardi Gras followed by Lent. A glorious pancake-fest followed by forty days of veganism and doleful thoughts of Jesus in the wilderness in the spring – balanced by a slap-up supper for the whole village in the autumn. November the tenth is sometimes called 'Martinmas Eve', because 11 November – which is the main bit of St Martin's Day, it having started the night before – kicks off the forty-day fast terrifying yourself with contemplation of the Last Judgment through Advent. And then Christmas to balance Easter. They laced the year up tight, those early missionaries. Joined-up thinking. Showing the connections. It wasn't just a random sequence strung together without thought."

Sid watches Rosie doodling on the edge of the scrap of paper as her mind dwells on these thoughts.

"People loved St Martin of Tours, didn't they?" she says. "He was a popular saint. A bit like St Nicholas in a way. Compassion and generosity. It goes down well."

"It does indeed. People liked his kindness – and that he was a quiet soul, who preferred to live simply. Another story they tell of St Martin is that when he was chosen to be a bishop, he didn't want to go. He hid in the goose-pen when they came to find him. The geese didn't come out of that one too well, because roast goose was added to the traditional Martinmas menu as a result – *Martinigansl*, they call it in Austria. But we don't have to pull out all the stops and have a roast. We could just settle for a couple of *rogal świętomarciński*."

Rosie looks at him blankly. "Some what?"

Sid grins at her.

"That's what they eat in Poland, on Martinmas Eve. No big deal. Croissants. Can we afford those?"

"You're on!" says Rosie. "Let's eat Polish tonight. The geese can live another day."

For sharing and wondering

- If you were preparing a special party feast, what would you include?
- Think of some examples of compromise being the means of achieving more.
- Is salvation about what we believe, what we do, or a mixture of both?

Into the Mystery

Loving God, in all our dealings with one another, help us to remember the wisdom of sharing and compromise, seeing the other person's point of view, remembering the need and wellbeing of the other. Help us to see that we all belong to one another, and that in working for the health and happiness of the community, we also ensure our own.

49

Feast of St Hilda of Whitby

"What d'you know about St Hilda of Whitby, Sid?" asks Rosie, as they stroll through the public gardens, equipped with a bag of brown bread to feed the birds this cold November day.

"Abbess Hilda?" Sid glances at her in surprise. "Why?"

"Today's her feast. Someone posted it on Facebook this morning. But I don't now anything about her at all. I don't even know much about Whitby – fishing village up in Yorkshire, isn't it?"

Sid nods. "That's right. It was in the North Riding – 'North Yorkshire' as they call it now – on the east coast; on the mouth of the River Esk. Cædmon lived there – the earliest English poet. He looked after the animals at the abbey, in the days of Abbess Hilda; Anglo-Saxon times, the seventh century. They call those years the Dark Ages, but that's only because we don't have as much information about life then as later. It wasn't a darkness of ignorance or immorality. On the contrary, it was a beautiful time in the British Isles, really; enlightened. A luminous time.

"We know about Cædmon and about Abbess Hilda both from Bede – the Venerable Bede as he's known – a monk at Jarrow who was born in the last decade of Abbess Hilda's life. He was called the 'Father of English History' because his greatest work was the *Historia ecclesiastica gentis Anglorum*, a history of the church and people in England. It runs to five books, and in the third one he tells of the Council of Whitby, a turning point for the church in England. Can we sit down a minute, Rosie? I'm puffed out, walking and talking!"

There's a bench looking down over the rose garden, nothing but twigs for the most part, now. Not many people have ventured out on this chilly day, so they sit under the bare trees, huddling close together against the cold. A squirrel watches them from a low branch, hopeful of something to eat. Sid, seeing it, throws the little animal a scrap of bread, which is seized gratefully.

"Abbess Hilda grew up in the court of King Edwin in Northumbria. She was baptized a Christian with all Edwin's household in a small wooden church near where York Minster stands today. The tradition of the church in those days was Celtic – brought from Iona by St Aidan, among others, and that was what Hilda knew, and what informed her as a Christian and later a nun, as well as the abbey she founded at Streanæshalch, later called Whitby. The monasticism of the Dark Ages was inspired faith community. The monasteries were like little villages – men and women could both join, some married some single. Even the abbots and abbesses might be married. As a faith tradition, it was rich in mysticism, philosophy and scholarship. Very imaginative, strongly tuned in to the natural world, respectful of women, artistic and poetic even where it was severe and ascetic, and rooted in the Scriptures.

"The Celtic church was committed to social justice, and to formation of Christian character. From Ireland came the tradition of the *anamchara* – the soul friend – a mentoring system still part of modern discipling. Kindness, hospitality, patience, self-discipline and inner strength, intimacy with God and cherishing of creation were all part of Celtic Christianity.

"Then came the Synod of Whitby, presided over by King Oswiu of Northumbria, convened to decide the official date of Easter.

"At that time, there were two strands in the British church – one arising from Iona, the other from Rome – and they had different ways of calculating the date of Easter, resulting in this most important feast being celebrated at different times depending which strand your church followed.

"The Ionan side wanted to uphold the traditions that had come down to them from St Columba, but the opposition espousing the Roman cause trumped them with the names of St Peter and St Paul, based at the church in Rome. King Oswiu asked if it were not the case that Christ had given St Peter the keys to the kingdom of heaven, declaring him to be the rock on which the church would be founded. When both sides concurred that this was so, King Oswiu decreed that the Roman method would henceforward be adopted. And this proved a pivotal moment in the life of the British church; a turning away from the mystical, poetical, organic thinking of the Celts to the more structured, organizational thought forms of the often distinctly misogynistic Roman church, based on papal authority and the Roman legal system.

"So, in my view at least, the Synod of Whitby was a sad day for the church in Britain. But Hilda herself was wise, and dearly loved. King Oswiu's choice of her monastery for the synod is an indication of its prestige. According to St Bede in his book, the ideals of Christian monasticism were upheld in Hilda's community: men and women worshipped together but lived separately; they studied the Scriptures; peace and charity characterized their lives; monks and nuns had no private property but the community held all goods in common. Something like the Shakers in eighteenth-century America.

"Hilda was consulted and esteemed by kings and religious leaders, held in the highest regard. But she had the common touch too, and it was not beneath her to listen with attention and respect to the lowliest people. That's how the poet Cædmon got his chance. Hilda listened to him and took seriously his visions and insights, when he was only the monastery cowherd.

"A wise woman, a gifted teacher and shrewd administrator, Hilda made her monastery into something of a centre of excellence. Five of her monks went on to become bishops. She was a person of great strength and energy, but she was loveable, not dominating; a woman of profound emotional intelligence. Bede says everyone who knew her called her mother because of her outstanding devotion and grace. And she ran her monastery in the Celtic style to the end of her life."

"The Celtic style? What would that mean?" asked Rosie.

"Well… she was a great one for education – she wanted both her monks and her nuns to be strengthened in wisdom and understanding. She prioritized peace, justice and sharing – simplicity – over power and hierarchical advancement. The Ionan monastics believed in living close to the earth – they took much of their inspiration from the Desert Fathers and Coptic Orthodoxy. They valued humility – a word that derives from 'earth'; same root as humus, or leaf-mould. The Romans were more into rank and power."

"Would things have been different, d'you think, if the vote had gone the other way at Whitby?"

Sid gets to his feet. The sky is overcast, and he thinks rain will fall before long. "Well," he says, as Rosie takes the hand he holds out to her and he pulls her up to stand beside him: "They say the Celtic church was serene and very pure in spirit. They went in for simplicity of life, intimacy with God, the equality of all people, and reverence for the living earth. They saw creation not as a challenge for domination, but as the outflowing poetry and music, the work of art, of a creator God. I do sometimes wonder if the consumerism we see today would have developed, without the decision of the Council of Whitby. It's hard to say."

"I wonder," Rosie muses, as they turn towards home, "if we could put it back?"

"Institutionally, not a chance; privately and personally, I don't see why not," says Sid. "It was a way that espoused fasting, silence and self-denial – yet for all that it was so life-affirming. It saw the hand of God in the beauty of the earth. I'd be up for that."

For sharing and wondering

- Think of some examples of female spiritual leaders, and why they have especially inspired you.
- What aspects of your faith would you be interested in studying further, and how might you go about this?
- Whether formally or informally, who has been a soul friend to you?

Into the Mystery

As we remember the teaching of Jesus that people would know by our love that we are his disciples, help us to celebrate and affirm one another, to make room for variety and difference, to listen to and encourage one another.

50

All Hallows

"Sid," says Rosie, "I wonder what it's *really* like to be dead. What happens? Honestly, I mean. I feel as though my mind has been… sort of *bullied* by the strong agendas of religious people. I suspect it's all mixed up with the reality that nobody can possibly say for certain what happens when we die, so the affiliates of religions have to come across extra certain to make up for that. But what do you think, Sid? What really happens? Does life just… end? Do we go on – and if we do, does our individuality continue, or is it like the Hindu nirvana? Does the form of the wave subside and the water inside it just merge with the ocean again? Do we come back? Do we learn and grow, still? Sid, I cannot believe it will really be all about singing choruses for ever and ever and ever in a huge glittering hall where the lights can't be turned off. That would be more like hell."

Sid looks up from his book. "How the heck would I know?"

"Oh, try, Sid! You must think something!"

"Whatever has put this into your mind anyway? Has someone died?"

"Hallowe'en. I was thinking about it. It's the Day of the Dead in Mexico, isn't it? How did the old Celts describe it? A thin time? Did they think spirits came back?"

Sid smiles at the picture the bombardment of questions brings to mind, of himself as an inexpert juggler trying in vain to keep all the balls in the air as enthusiastic onlookers throw him more and more.

"Samhain," he says, "yes; the cross-quarter day midway between the autumn equinox and the winter solstice. It marked the end of the Celtic year, and I think that's why it came to be their day of the dead – like the Mexicans. The year was dying, the people looked back and remembered – and paid their respects to – their beloved dead. Interestingly, similar to the November observance of the fallen in war at Armistice Day. And, yes, they thought Samhain was a 'thin time' – an occasion when the veil between the physical universe and the unseen world, that the ancient Celts knew as the Realm of Weird, was exceptionally thin. A time to be close to all those one had loved and lost.

"The early missionaries settled the celebration of All Saints on that sacred festival, making the connection between familial kindred mourned and remembered, and the great company of the faithful, the cloud of witnesses – the church universal. And this observance began at sundown on 31 October, remember – because the Celtic day did not begin in the morning. It started at sundown – like the Jewish day, and probably others too that I don't know about.

"So the ancient Celts understood dreams not as processing the day gone, but as preparation for the day coming. Thinking about Joseph (of the amazing technicolour dreamcoat fame) and the other Joseph (husband of Mary the mother of Jesus), it seems they thought of dreams in the same way – anticipatory. So the beginning of Samhain was what came to be known as 'All Hallows Eve' (or Hallowe'en), 'Hallows' being another word for 'Holy Ones', going on into what we now call All Saints Day on 1 November. That was how the old Celtic observance of the unity of the seen and unseen worlds was baptized into Christian practice.

"That's easy enough to describe, but what really happens when we die is another question entirely. I'm going to make a cup of tea while I think about it. Can I get you one as well?"

He brings the steaming mugs back to the fireside, and settles down into his easy chair again.

"I think," he says slowly, "that you kind of shut yourself out of understanding eternal life if you try to think of it as linear – because it isn't. Eternal life isn't chronological. My belief – and please, this is only me – is that the cross of Christ sits at the heart of creation; you know, that thing in the Bible, how God was in Christ reconciling all things to himself. That the cross of Jesus restored the cosmos to peace?[114] Even if it doesn't always feel like it – the solution is in place now as well as all the problems.

"And I think life organizes around that central event, rooted in it, drawn to it – all the limitless possibilities both within time and beyond it."

He sips his tea, cautious because it is still hot. "You see, to me, Rosie, death is not a state, it's more an event – the one that balances birth. The context of both of them is life. And there's that old saying, 'Where there's life, there's hope.' In the context of life, anything is possible. And there is always life, because life proceeds from God, and God is the context of… everything. So what happens when we're dead is not a question I ask myself, because it's all about doorways – the present moment is the doorway to eternal life, and death is only one of many moments, many doorways leading in.

"Heaven, hell, life on Earth, life hereafter, they are all in a sense the same – I think, Rosie, this is just me thinking aloud – but I think they must be, because there is nowhere to be but God, no power but God. To talk of life or experience outside God means nothing, it's a contradiction in terms. The thing to concentrate on is always the same – the cross of Christ at the heart of creation, holding everything together in unity. Our certain hope.

"There is a sort of deadness, of course, in outmoded forms. The empty shells of snails the blackbird has eaten. The transparent shed skins of snakes. Cuttlefish bones on the seashore. They are part of what has gone; their usefulness now is in the endless transmutation of life's forms. They have to be taken up into the new creation. I

114 Colossians 1:20.

suspect religious institutions come into the same category. The skin and bone of something vital for a while, then empty, brittle, hollow, dry – waiting to be drawn up into the purposes of life again, in a new way."

"Perhaps that's true of an individual human life too," says Rosie.

"Maybe." Sid frowns. "But I don't think so. It's true of the body, of course, but not of the soul. Religious institutions are the body of faith, not its soul, so they wear out, they lose their usefulness in that particular form. I mean, don't they call the church 'the body of Christ'? But the soul, the living core – whether of an individual or the ardent, hopeful flame of the gospel itself – can never be lost. That would be an intrinsic impossibility. Because it came from the breath of God, and belongs to God's Spirit for ever."

For sharing and wondering

- Are you more of a loner, or do you enjoy being part of a group?
- What forms of remembrance do you find especially meaningful?
- What do you believe happens to us when we die?

Into the Mystery

Sometimes we feel so lost and lonely, Lord – life is so vast and puzzling. Our small ship sails with such fragility on this huge and fathomless sea. Be our guiding star, be the wind in our sails. Let us not miss our way. Bring us safely home.

51

No Time

"Come on," says Rosie, "we've been talking about going for a walk every day this week. We'll lose the use of our muscles if we sit here vegetating much longer. We ought to get up off our rapidly enlarging behinds and take some exercise. It's a beautiful day. There's no time like the present. Let's go."

So they do.

The gales of recent storms have shaken many trees in the park bare of leaves, and the paths underfoot are carpeted with gold as a result. Every dip and hollow has its puddle, and the lichen on the wet bark glows in rich colour in the morning sun. Everywhere, birds are singing. The day is lovely.

"There's a real nip in the air, now," says Sid. "I'm starting to believe in winter."

Rosie doesn't answer this conversational remark. She is deep in thought, her hands thrust into the warmth of her pockets as she strolls along. Sid waits for her to begin to tell him what she's thinking about, which – eventually – she does.

"I can remember a day," she says, "when I first *heard* spiders. Somebody had told me spiders click to each other. And then one summer I got a tummy bug, with a high fever, and for three days I couldn't get out of bed. I was eighteen years old, volunteering on a children's project based in an old farmhouse, so I lay upstairs on a bed – I think the room had no other furniture, it was peaceful, empty, bare, painted white and full of summer light; I loved it. Where the walls met the ceiling, in every corner, a spider. Those ballet spiders – you know, Sid? The ones with tiny round bodies and long, dancing, delicate legs."

"*Pholcus phalangioides*," says Sid. "Daddy-long-legs."

"Oh!" Rosie looks at him. "I thought a daddy-long-legs was a crane fly. Anyway, never mind – you know the ones I mean. So, when I was in bed those three days, drifting in fever, I heard the spiders clicking to each other. I suppose they just got used to me lying there. I expect normally when someone comes in they stop talking, and wait in watching silence for them to leave.

"And I was thinking – I know it doesn't often happen that a person gets to lie still for three days, but I'm so grateful that I did. It was forty years ago, and I can still remember the quiet of that spacious room with its simple low bed and expanses of summer light, and the spiders clicking. I've been asking myself, why do I have no time any more? As a child, as a teenager, I had time to watch and dream and think, time to listen. But ever since I grew up, I've had no time.

"I try to tell myself I've been busy, but it isn't that. When the children were little, I just sat around minding them while they played – I had chores to do, but nothing mega. My work has often been quiet and solitary – cleaning people's houses while they were out at work, doing night duties as a care assistant in nursing homes, that sort of thing. But even so, I've felt under pressure most of my life. To make ends meet, to come up to expectations, to look busy because other people were. And the aggregate of all that has amounted to feeling as though I always had no time. Which I might as well not have done if I can't settle into the time I have, in peace."

They come to the steps cut into the steepness of the hillside, and go single file down to the lower level of the park, by the bandstand and the rose garden. The small streams that flow the length of this spit of land, swollen with the autumn rain, go tumbling and gurgling alongside the path.

"No Time," says Sid, "is what we're in."

Rosie looks at him. "Explain."

"No Time. Do you remember? It's the part of the Celtic wheel of the year that comes between Samhain and Yul.[115] After the day of the dead and before the new infant light seed is born. No Time is the quintessential space. It's like the gap between Jesus dying and rising again, when he lay in the tomb – busy, according to Christian legend, harrowing hell; but who knows? He just lay still. It's like those three days you took aside from the bustle of things with the sunlight and spiders, healing. They were brilliant, those ancient Celts, Rosie. How utterly wise, to understand that every cycle of life, every year, soul, needs its No Time – not *for* anything, just space in between things, space to just be.

"You know that famous passage from the Bible, *to everything there is a time*… no… *to everything*… how does it go?"

"'To everything there is a season, and a time to every purpose under heaven.' I can always remember," says Rosie, "because back in the 1970s Mary Hopkin had a single that went to the top of the charts, 'Those Were The Days'. And on the B-side she recorded the song 'Turn Turn Turn', about the changing seasons, the turning circle, of a person's life. It was basically that passage from Ecclesiastes embellished a bit and set to music.[116] When I can't remember how the quote goes, I run that song in my mind, and then I can – 'To everything (turn, turn, turn), there is a season (turn, turn, turn) and a time to every purpose under heaven.' Ooh, Sid! I wonder if it was a Shaker song in the first place?"

"Sounds like it, doesn't it – but no, Pete Seeger wrote it in the 1950s. I know the one you mean. Anyway, that thing it says, *to everything there is a purpose and a time for every season*… no, wait, I've got it muddled up again."

"Never mind," says Rosie: "I know what you mean."

"OK. Well it's a kind of 'time and a place for everything' passage,

115 To cross-reference for Samhain and Yul, see chapters 1, 5, 50.
116 Ecclesiastes 3:1.

obviously. And generally speaking, that is how religious people live. The observant life – by which I mean not the life that notices things but the one dedicated to religious observance – is always occupied. You know – 'The devil finds things for idle hands to do' as they used to say, and John Wesley never letting himself be without occupation. He accounted for every hour in every day, scrupulously. Even a 'quiet time' is an occupation, packed tight with Bible study and thanksgiving and intercession and confession and the Lord knows what else.

"Well, the Celtic wheel of the year, especially because it's rooted in farming, is also tightly tied to occupation in a way – Martinmas is time to slaughter the beasts, Imbolc is time to sweep out the house after the winter, Lammas is time to start the harvest and Mabon is time to conclude it. But what an absolute divine inspiration to leave a fallow field, a little sabbath, an undesignated space. No Time. Brilliant. Everyone who finds they have no time needs No Time."

"So No Time," Rosie checks, "is what we're in right now?"

"That's right. We are."

"Ha!" says Rosie. "How cool is that! Exactly what I need."

For sharing and wondering

- What different jobs or occupations have you done at different times of your life?
- What activities make you feel peaceful and happy?
- In what ways can you build a sabbath principle of restorative space into the regular routines of your life?

Into the Mystery

Breathe your peace into our hearts, Spirit of God. Help us to centre ourselves in your love. Restore in us the joy of your salvation. Give us the grace in every single day to connect with the pure joy of your presence. May all that you are flow steadily through all that we are, transforming us into the likeness of Jesus our Lord.

52

Feast of Christ the King

"I'm frankly not too sure how this happens," says Sid. "How you can be rolling along, doing the stuff like you've been taught, giving it your best shot and getting it more or less right – and then suddenly it all starts to unravel. Maybe an illness catches you unawares, or someone has a traffic accident, or a child is born with serious health issues. Maybe somebody close to you commits a crime, or you do something majorly silly yourself – some huge indiscretion or massive mistake. And you're down.

"If you're one of those people who write best-selling testimony books, you see the light and find Jesus, you come fighting back and the empire you build second time round is all wise and beautiful and sure to last – unlike the poor tawdry efforts of the first one before you got converted.

"But... there are those of us who can't write and haven't really got a story much to tell. We did our best, it came unstuck, we lost what we had. And we're down, we never do manage to get it together after that. We just never get up again. I guess some people aren't fighters is what it comes down to. All the promise and potential comes to nothing; and afterwards it's a matter of getting by. Bumping along the bottom. Making ends meet and not thinking too much about tomorrow.

"Not that life is all bad – it's not dramatic, not a matter of anguish and suffering. What was that thing George Borrow said?[117] 'There's

117 In his book Lavengro, 1851.

night and day, brother, both sweet things; sun, moon, and stars, brother, all sweet things; there's likewise a wind on the heath. Life is very sweet, brother; who would wish to die?'

"But aspirations change. You start out set to conquer the world, and by the end you have to be glad if it hasn't conquered you.

"I have to say, if I'm honest, it's partly why I find Quaker meeting such a refuge. They most of them don't show many signs of knowing what the Bible says. See, I read the parable of the talents, about the Master coming back and requiring an account from his servants of the talents they were given. And guess which one I identify with? The guy who lost his nerve, buried what he had in the dust, and had nothing to show for what had been entrusted to him. And the Master was angry, and threw him out – abandoned him to devastation… outer darkness… alienation. Because he wasted what he had. He lost his courage. He was down, and he never got up again. But they don't talk about that kind of thing at Quaker meeting. They just sit quietly. I've heard some people find the silence harrowing because it sifts the depths, but I don't mind that. Many a midnight has searched the bowels of my soul. I can live with that. But what… Rosie, what if I am one of those rejected? If there really is a day of reckoning, and the Master looks at me and says 'You should have done better, Sid. I gave you so much. You lived in a time of peace in one of the richest and most comfortable nations on the Earth. You had every chance. I'm sorry, old chum, you blew it. I'd like to say it was nice knowing you, but the truth is we never did really know each other; if we had, you'd have made a better fist of it than you did. Sid, you never even tried.' What if it all ends like that? And what if it *doesn't* end? If there really is a hell, and it is eternal?"

Rosie listens carefully to this. She knows the territory all too well, and she has no easy answers to lift away the uncertainties, the doubt and the despair. She listens, and she waits. In any circumstance of life, Rosie can only ever think of one thing – whatever is the truth as it appears to her in that given situation. This has made her unpopular at times, because she can never think of anything more suitable or more diplomatic. Her honest response fills her mind; and nothing else comes. Right now, she can think of only one thing, so she says it quietly and hopes it doesn't sound too pious or religious.

"Jesus said: 'Come unto me all you who are burdened and struggling, and I will give you rest. Take my yoke upon you and learn from me. I am gentle and humble of heart – lowly. Your soul will find rest, with me. My yoke is easy, and my burden is light.'[118] Jesus, Sid... well, I guess the main thing he did was come here to be with us. It wasn't so much about how high he could rise as how low he could stoop. He came to find us. Not like Spiderman abseiling down a skyscraper, but just a baby whose mother was in one hell of a mess. You know, he cannot possibly have had a plan. I mean, babies don't plan anything, do they? Endlessly demanding, completely unreasonable – eat, scream, dirty their nappies, sleep (if you're lucky), and rely on you to give them a cuddle. That was the beginning of our salvation. The nearest thing that Jesus had to a plan.

"Because of my depression, and because I could never really make it in the mainstream, I've had to content myself with just reaching out for something good in any given day. Whatever comes to hand and seems like a good idea at the time. One foot in front of the other. The journey of a thousand miles begins with a single step.[119]

"And I have to tell you, Sid, one of the best things I ever reached out for was you. When I was a girl and got married the first time, it never crossed my mind it wouldn't be forever. Divorce wasn't an option, but it happened to me nonetheless. And it hasn't escaped my attention that the Bible calls the love between you and me adultery. Two divorced people with the temerity to get up and start again. But I don't call it adultery. I call it grace. I call it a second chance.

"I know you unravelled, Sid. I think that's OK. What could I have loved in you if you'd been invulnerable? What part could you have had in me if you'd been a shiny success?

118 Matthew 11:28–30, my paraphrase,
119 Reference Lao Tsu, the Tao Te Ching, chapter 64.

"Maybe, in the days when you were down, God looked at you and scratched his holy head and asked Jesus, 'What the dickens are we going to do with him now?' And maybe Jesus said 'Heh heh, just you wait. I've got a job for that guy. I've been wondering who on earth would look after my Rosie.'

"Sid, if all you ever did was walk alongside me and be my lover and my friend, keep me from topping myself and forgive me all my bitching and perennial craziness, I think that would be enough for God. I mean he set the bar low – sending a kid with no dad, no home and no money and hoping that would do to save the world. Geez, Sid! Surely he can cope with you and me!"

For sharing and wondering

- In what ways do you think your life experiences have changed you?
- Thinking of your own life, what are the particular things you believe God put you on Earth to do?
- In difficult times, what have you found has helped to sustain your faith?

Into the Mystery

Oh God grant us thy peace,
the peace of men also,
the peace of St Columba the kind,
and of St Mary mild, the loving one,
and of Christ, the king of the human heart.[120]

---

120 Celtic prayer. I cannot now find the source, but I think it may be attributable to Alastair MacLean – if you know, please contact the publisher so we can credit properly in future editions.

Appendix

Sid's recipe for lemon cheesecake

For the topping:
- 4 tablespoons water
- ½ oz (15 g) powdered gelatin
- 3 large eggs
- 4 oz (125 g) caster sugar
- Finely grated rind and juice of two lemons
- 1lb (500 g) fresh cream cheese (or any soft, white cheese)
- 1 carton (6 fl. oz, 175 ml) double cream

For the crumb base:
- 8 digestive biscuits
- 1 level tablespoon caster sugar
- 2 oz (50 g) butter

Measure the water into a saucepan, sprinkle in the gelatin and set aside to soak for five minutes, then stir over a low heat until the gelatin has dissolved and draw off the heat ready to use.

Separate the eggs, putting the yolks in one mixing bowl and the whites in a second, larger mixing bowl.

Add the sugar, finely grated lemon rind and lemon juice to the yolks. Set the mixing bowl over a saucepan half-filled with simmering water and whisk until the mixture is frothy and light in colour. Remove from the heat and whisk in the dissolved gelatin. Blend the cream cheese until smooth, and then gradually whisk in the gelatin and egg mixture (best on a machine). Beat the mixture well until thick and light – by now it will almost be set.

Lightly whip the cream and stiffly beat the egg whites (adding a little sugar to the egg whites during this process is good – it means any unblended incidence of beaten egg-white encountered while eating the cheesecake tastes sweet not revolting). Fold both into the setting cheese mixture, gently but thoroughly.

Pour into an 8-inch round loose-bottomed cake tin lined on the base with a circle of greaseproof paper.

Crush the digestive biscuits and mix with the sugar. Melt the butter and stir in the crumbs with a fork. Spoon over the top of the cheesecake mixture, and chill until quite firm.

To freeze: Cover with foil and freeze. Remove from tin, wrap in foil and replace in freezer.

To serve: If frozen, unwrap, put on serving dish, thaw overnight in fridge.

Goes well with summer berries or strawberry sauce.

Also by Penelope Wilcock

"Clear, provocative, focused, and accessible, these pithy studies are a treasure-trove for home groups and other discussion-based gatherings. The range is inspiring – a tour of the Bible in 100 bites. Recommended!"

– GERARD KELLY, THE BLESS NETWORK

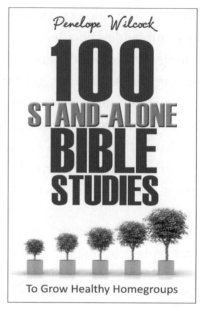

To Grow Healthy Homegroups

These studies provide a bridge for people to find their place in the Bible story. Designed to be used individually, they can also be followed thematically – with twenty-five studies on Bible characters; twenty lessons from the life of Jesus; five studies from the Law and Prophets; and more. Each double-page spread has a Bible passage, supporting commentary, a series of questions, and a prayer.

"Have fun with these outlines," writes Pen Wilcock. "May your home be a place of friendship, somewhere people can learn to love the Lord Jesus, a safe place to become more self-aware and awake to the beauty and the vulnerability of their fellow-pilgrims."

"Pen Wilcock has done it again! She gets to the heart of the truth in a way that fills the imagination, challenges the heart and gives you a desire not just to think about faith but do something. These studies will have home groups talking for hours."

– MALCOLM DUNCAN, GOLD HILL BAPTIST CHURCH

MONARCH

ISBN 978-0-85721-419-5 £12.99
Monarch
www.lionhudson.com

Jesus said his burden is light. It doesn't always feel that way.

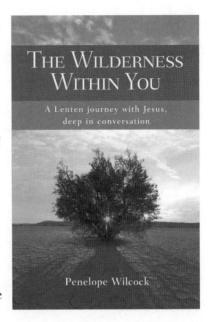

What does he mean when he says "take up your cross"?
Is it a metaphor? Is he serious? Or, "If you do not give up everything, you cannot be my disciple." What?

Following Jesus is not so simple as preachers make out. So Pen sets out into the wilderness to look for him. She wants to ask him some questions.

Somewhat to her surprise, she meets him one wet morning, crossing the road in her home town...

"Pen approaches the spiritual journey like a jungle explorer, and documents it with the sparkling prose of a good travel writer. She trades doctrine for delight and religion for relationship in a narrative peppered with the kinds of insights that only come when the imagination is engaged."
– GERARD KELLY, AUTHOR OF *CHURCH ACTUALLY* AND CO-FOUNDER OF THE BLESS NETWORK

MONARCH
ISBN 978-0-85721-497-3 £7.99
Monarch
www.lionhudson.com

VOLUME
ONE

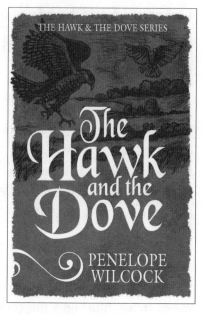

The Hawk and the Dove

PENELOPE WILCOCK

Father Peregrine is appointed Abbot of St Alcuin's Benedictine abbey. An arrogant, impatient man, a hawk trying hard to be a dove – his name in religion is "Columba" – he is respected, but not loved.

A sudden, shocking act of violence changes everything. As the story unfolds, this community of monks, serious about their calling but as flawed and human as we are, come to love their ascetic but now vulnerable leader.

They lived six centuries ago, yet their struggles are our own. Finding our niche; coping with failure; living with impossible people; and discovering that we are the impossible ones.

"Not to be missed."
MEL STARR

"Poignant, moving, rich with imagery and emotion... Modern readers will easily identify with each character in Wilcock's timeless human drama. Highly recommended reading."
MIDWEST BOOK REVIEW

ISBN 978-1-78264-139-1 £7.99
Lion Fiction
www.lionhudson.com